Strategic Market Planning

Strategic Market Planning:
The Pursuit of Competitive Advantage

George S. Day
University of Toronto

West Publishing Company

St. Paul   New York   Los Angeles   San Francisco

COPYRIGHT © 1984 By WEST PUBLISHING CO.
610 Opperman Drive
P.O. Box 64526
St. Paul, MN 55164–0526

Printed in the United States of America

95   94   8

Library of Congress Cataloging in Publication Data

Day, George S.
  Strategic market planning.

  Includes index.
  1. Corporate planning. 2. Marketing research.
3. Competition. I. Title.
HD30.28.D39 1984   658.4'012   84–2282
ISBN 0–314–77884–5

To Marilyn

Contents

Developing Strategy Options: The Role of Generic Strategies   5

Creative Thinking about Strategy Options   6

7 *Evaluating the Strategic Options*   *151*

Implementing Strategic Decisions   *181*   8

Summary: Meeting the Challenges of Strategic Market Planning   *205*   9

Bibliography   *215*

Preface

The purpose of this preface is to provide the prospective reader a bridge from the title to the chapters that follow. The title has three distinct components that are also major themes that have shaped the contents of this book.

Market strategies. Our focus is on the long-run courses of action that a business takes within the markets it elects to serve. This means we are dealing with broader issues than the activities of the separate functions, for market strategies are most effective when they engage the total capabilities of the business. Within this context, however, marketing is the predominant general management function, for it plays the leading role in keeping the business in step with the anticipated market environment.

Planning. The second theme is the value of a systematic process for relating the competencies of the business with the threats and opportunities in the market environment. The process followed in this book puts a premium on the explicit development of strategy alternatives and on the fostering of strategic thinking about the future prospects for the business.

No strategy—regardless of how well conceived and appropriate it may be—will have an impact unless there is a commitment to action and a close coupling of the strategy with operations and implementation programs. One of the best ways to achieve this commitment is to have continuing participation of key functional managers in the development of the strategies, coupled with a productive top-down and bottom-up dialogue. Effective strategies should reflect a blend of top-down corporate concerns, with resource allocation and profit performance, and bottom-up understanding of specific product-market opportunities.

Competitive advantage. This theme provides the logic by which the disparate concerns of different functional managers are integrated. Each function can serve the business best by uniting with other functions to create and sustain a meaningful advantage over the competition. Until recently, the benefits of this integrating logic were not being realized because of the practical problems of applying the concept. Fortunately, there is now a considerable body of research and applications experience we can draw on to help surmount these problems.

Strategic market planning. By combining the three themes, we arrive at a working definition of the topic of this book:

.   .   . strategic marketing planning is a

.   .   . process that encourages and guides the dialogue between functions and organization levels

.   .   . on how a business unit can best compete in the markets it elects to serve.

This definition has also guided the structure of this book, which follows the basic steps of the strategic planning process. The first two chapters describe the evolution of planning practice and amplify the meaning of competitive strategies. The third chapter introduces the planning process and the basic elements of the situation assessment. The fourth chapter looks more thoroughly at the market analysis and definition component of the situation analysis. Chapters 5 and 6 mark the transition from a focus on understanding the current situation to a consideration of the future possibilities. Two approaches to generating options are considered. One looks for inspirations from generalized game plans; the other looks for specific routes to competitive advantage that are grounded in the specifics of the market situation and capabilities of the business. Chapter 7 establishes the criteria for evaluating strategies and guiding the choice from among the set of feasible options. Chapters 8 and 9 deal with the translation of the strategic decision into a course of action and address the challenges of implementation.

This book is designed for two audiences. The first is *managers* seeking a systematic approach to apply to the difficult problem of adapting their businesses to fast-changing competitive environments. Much of the material in this book was developed to provide resource materials for line managers and staff planners and analysts who were working together in planning sessions to formulate and evaluate the strategic options for their business.

The second audience is *students* of management with a good knowledge of the basics of marketing at the brand or product level but only a passing familiarity with contemporary strategy concepts. For this audience, the book is designed to serve as the basic text for both executive development programs in strategic marketing and graduate or advanced undergraduate courses in planning, marketing management, or strategic market planning. This book has proven to be a very effective conceptual framework for courses with a heavy orientation toward case analysis.

The West Series on Strategic Market Management

While this book can be used on its own, it is also the first in a planned series of five books.

The second book in the series will cover the strategy analysis methods used in support of the planning process, such as portfolio models and the analysis of pooled business experience from the PIMS (Profit Impact of Market Strategies) project. An important feature of this book will be the emphasis on the conceptual underpinnings of these methods—notably experience effects, the market share-profitability relationship, and the product life cycle.

The remaining books in the series will cover such topics as the organization and control of marketing activities and the strategic management of new products, and will also provide more thorough coverage of the analysis of markets, competitors, and channel members. While each of these books can be treated as a distinct module in a course, they are all designed to be used within the basic framework established by this first book.

Acknowledgments

Many people have contributed directly and indirectly to the formulation of the ideas in this book. I am especially indebted to the consulting clients who have given me the opportunity to apply the planning process described in this book to more than thirty business units in a variety of industry environments ranging from household security systems and automotive parts to financial services and telecommunications equipment. These experiences have strongly reinforced my belief that operating managers are in the best position to articulate the strategy options for a business.

Many friends and colleagues have been influential in shaping my thinking about strategy. Special thanks are due to those who also commented extensively on various drafts of this book, including David Montgomery of Stanford, Barton Weitz of Wharton, and Robin Wensley of the University of London. Numerous others will recognize their ideas and concepts at various points in this book, for the field of strategy has progressed through unselfish sharing of experience. I wish I could properly acknowledge each of you.

My greatest debt is to my wife, who understands the rigors of writing and provided a supportive and caring environment for this undertaking.

George S. Day

Strategic Market Planning

The Nature of Strategic Market Planning

Chapter 1

{ Successful organizations follow a strategy that describes the *direction* the organization will pursue within its chosen environment, and guides the *allocation* of resources and effort. Without a strategy, an organization is like a ship without a rudder, condemned to wander aimlessly in response to winds, currents, and outside events. Since the outside pressures in a competitive market are seldom benign, the consequences of a poorly considered strategy can be disastrous.[1] }

A strategy also provides a logic that *integrates* the parochial perspectives of functional departments and operating units, and points them all in the same direction. Otherwise, each function will do what it thinks important or serves its immediate interests. The pressures from different reward structures, time horizons, and educational backgrounds are often overwhelming and potentially dysfunctional unless channeled.

Pressures for Formal Strategic Planning. Until recently it was possible to prosper in many industries with a trial-and-error approach to planning. Essentially, this approach meant continuing with programs and activities that seemed to be working and eliminating or changing those that were not working. The strategy was not explicit; instead, it was fully understood only after the fact, when an attempt was made to interpret the patterns in the stream of decisions taken piecemeal during the previous year. The key planning assumption was that the rate of change in the environment would be slower than the response time. In environments shaped by intense competition, discontinuities in key economic trends, and compressed time horizons, however, this approach is frequently too costly in terms of missed opportunities.

---

1. Ross and Kami (1973).

Rapid environmental change and increasing uncertainty have put a premium on strategies that anticipate and shape events rather than simply respond to them. Firms have accepted this challenge in many ways. Their responses, and the accumulated knowledge and experience, have established what is currently meant by strategic planning. This process has two related manifestations: one at the corporate level and the other at the business unit or division level. Our focus in this book will be at the business unit level, for this level is where market-oriented strategies for competitive advantage are pursued.

This chapter sets the stage for the rest of the book by dealing with such questions as, What is meant by strategic market planning? What is the process and orientation that yields a strategic market plan to carry out all aspects of a business's strategy within the market arenas where it elects to compete? The answers to these questions will change as the environment of business imposes new demands. In the last section, therefore, we review the evolution of strategic planning practice to its present form.

Perspectives on Strategic Planning

The essence of strategic planning is the consideration of current decision alternatives in light of their probable consequences over time. This means identifying foreseeable threats to avoid and opportunities to pursue. Two implications of this perspective are especially important. First, strategic planning is not a way of avoiding or minimizing risks. If anything, it should increase risk taking by ensuring that possible risks are considered and better contained. Second, strategic planning does not require a superior crystal ball in an attempt to outwit the future. The future is unpredictable, but it is not a random walk. Strong likelihoods, built-in dynamics, and even a few near-certainties are present in each market. Thus, strategic planning is the effective application of the best available information to decisions that have to be made now to ensure a secure future.

Strategic planning does not deal with future decisions. It deals with the futurity of present decisions.

—Peter Drucker

No single definition has been able to capture all facets of contemporary strategic planning practice. Four distinguishing features, however, shape the accepted meaning:

- an external orientation,
- a process for formulating strategies,

- methods for the analysis of strategic situations and alternatives, and
- a commitment to action.

External Orientation:
The Strategic Role of Marketing

The primary responsibility of strategic planning is to look continuously outward and keep the business in step with the anticipated environment. The lead role in meeting this responsibility is played by marketing, for this is the boundary function between the firm and its customers, distributors, and competitors. As a general management responsibility, marketing embraces the interpretations of the environment and the crucial choices of customers to serve, competitors to challenge, and the product characteristics with which the business will compete. Strategic market planning is broader than marketing, however, for strategies that start with the analysis of market responses will not be effective unless they are fully integrated with other functional decisions.

Chance favors the prepared mind.

—Louis Pasteur

Organizations do not naturally adopt an external or market orientation. The persistent tendency is to be inner directed and to give unbalanced emphasis to internal aspirations and short-run efficiency considerations. Organizations forget the need to be externally oriented at their peril. Even companies that excel at strategic planning can lose sight of the primacy of marketing. John Welch, the chief executive officer (CEO) of General Electric, strongly made this point as he reflected on his organization's experience:

> The desire for sure things, and the long-view vacuum left by marketing, brought on strategic planning. At financial planning, at resource allocation—the internalities—strategic planning did well; but not too well at marketing—the crucial externality. Comfortable with quantification, strategic planning mapped the external world beautifully—market size and share, it made huge contributions to resource allocation . . . but strategic planning didn't or couldn't chart a market course. It didn't navigate . . . it didn't lead . . . and unfortunately, too often it was seen to replace marketing.[2]

An effective market orientation is not simply a customer orientation that implies a battle for ultimate customers—a battle won by direct appeal to these customers. Instead, the perspective must be

---

2. Welch (1982).

broadened to view customers as an ultimate "prize" gained at the expense of competitors in many ways other than by simply offering a better match of products to customer needs. Additional sources of advantage over competitors can be found in strong distribution arrangements, lower costs, proprietary technology, and so forth.

Strategy Formulation Process

Strategies are the product of a special kind of problem-solving activity. As a result, most strategic planning processes share the same basic steps. Finding a planning process that did not have at least the following steps would be unusual: (1) situation assessment (including specifying the current strategy), (2) setting objectives, (3) generating and evaluating strategy alternatives, (4) selecting the best strategy, (5) developing detailed plans to make sure the strategies will achieve the established objectives, (6) implementation, and (7) performance monitoring.

We are all continually faced with a series of great opportunities brilliantly disguised as insoluble problems.

—John W. Gardner

Where planning processes differ most is the sequence in which the steps are followed.[3] The *management by objectives* (MBO) approach begins by developing a comprehensive list of goals and objectives. The next task is to generate alternative strategies for achieving the objectives. The difficulty with this approach is that objectives tend to be unrealistic because they do not consider the environment or capabilities of the business. Another planning sequence, the *inside-outside* approach, starts with the organization's resources and then asks what can be achieved with them. While this approach is useful for businesses that have a unique opportunity or a protected leadership position, it may also lead to unrealistic assessments of the capacity of the firm to compete. An unfortunate tendency with this approach is to look at the environment from the vantage point of the business strengths without giving due attention to unfavorable aspects of the environment.

This book will follow a third sequence of steps, which has been called the *strategic thinking* approach. The essence of this approach is the generation of feasible strategy alternatives in light of the external environment and the capabilities of the organization. This step is followed by an assessment of the outcomes of these alternatives in light of risks, costs, and rewards, which in turn yields objectives that can be realistically achieved. This process is outlined in Figure 1.1, which also shows how this sequence has been used to organize the structure of this book.

---

3. A similar argument can be found in Rothschild (1976).

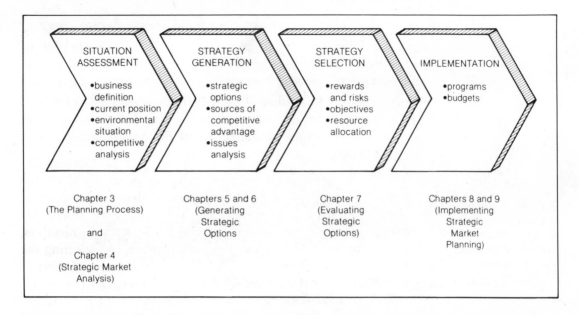

SITUATION ASSESSMENT	STRATEGY GENERATION	STRATEGY SELECTION	IMPLEMENTATION
•business definition •current position •environmental situation •competitive analysis	•strategic options •sources of competitive advantage •issues analysis	•rewards and risks •objectives •resource allocation	•programs •budgets
Chapter 3 (The Planning Process) and Chapter 4 (Strategic Market Analysis)	Chapters 5 and 6 (Generating Strategic Options)	Chapter 7 (Evaluating Strategic Options)	Chapters 8 and 9 (Implementing Strategic Market Planning)

The strategic planning process seldom resembles a tidy, linear sequence with a clear-cut beginning and endpoint. The process does, however, eventually yield a set of plans. Because these plans are partially implemented through a regular budgeting cycle, they are usually completed with that schedule in mind. Just as the environment is continually changing, however, so is strategic planning a continuously evolving process. What must be sought is a strategic orientation to environmental change so that when action is taken, it will reinforce rather than compromise the basic thrust of the strategy.

Figure 1.1 Overview of Strategic Planning Process

Strategy Analysis Methods

The third significant dimension of contemporary strategic planning practice is the development of methods to facilitate the generation, structuring, and evaluation of strategies. Progress has been made in three related areas:

Beware of the handwriting on the wall; it may be a forgery.

—Herman Kahn

1. Planning concepts and techniques:
   - Market segmentation and product positioning analysis, directed to the identification of distinct customer groups and opportunities for differentiated competitive positions.
   - Product life-cycle analysis, which provides a systematic framework for examining market dynamics.

- The influence of experience and scale economies on changes in industry cost structures over time, and the cost position of competitors.

2. Analytical planning methods:

   - Portfolio classification and analysis models using two-dimensional displays to compare businesses and products in terms of the attractiveness of the market and the strength of competitive position.

   - Analysis of pooled business experience (the PIMS approach), which permits a business to learn from *strategy peers* who are conducting a large number of strategy experiments from a similar competitive position, rather than from *industry peers* who participate in the same industry but face different strategic situations.

3. Strategic assumption surfacing and testing:

   - A variety of methods have been developed to aid the identification of strategic issues and assumptions. These are not analytical techniques per se, but are methods for enhancing the process of planning.

These methods and concepts can play an important role in supporting management judgment by simplifying and structuring complex situations. They are, however, not a substitute for strategic thinking grounded in the realities of the particular situation.

Commitment to Action:
The Need for Top-Down and Bottom-Up Dialogue

The output of strategic planning is decisions, implemented by operating managers acting roughly in concert to carry out a strategy they helped devise. Documented plans, analyses, forecasts, and objectives are only a means to that end, for of themselves they have little impact on the ongoing activities of the business.

The decisions themselves will lose impact and support to the extent they reflect a predominance of top-down or bottom-up perspectives on the issues confronting the business. The challenge is to foster a dialogue that blends the top-down corporate concerns with resource allocations and long-run industry position, with the bottom-up understanding of specific-product market opportunities. The decisions taken need not have full concensus—a rare occurrence. It is critical, however, that all operating managers understand why the strategic direction was chosen and have a substantial commitment to changing their functional activities in line with the strategy.

The Evolution of Strategic Planning

Planning systems evolve in response to changing environmental conditions and managerial problems.[4]   Formal strategic planning—and business-level planning in particular—is simply the latest in a continuing series of advances in practice.   This progression can be segmented into three sequential phases, which are summarized in Figure 1.2: (1) budget-based planning, (2) long-range planning, and (3) strategic planning.

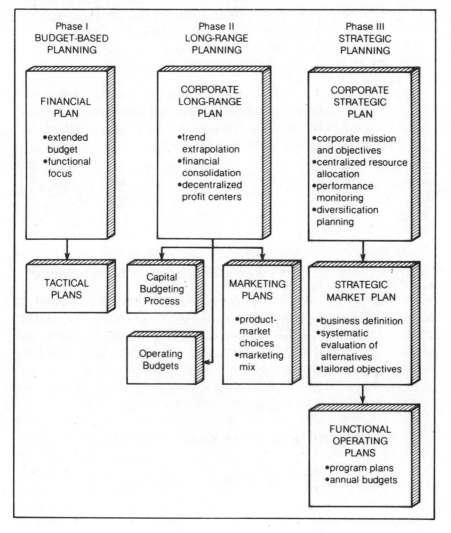

Figure 1.2 The Evolution of Strategic Planning

---

4. Ansoff (1980).

A fourth phase, called strategic management, is now emerging to address the changing conditions of the eighties and the abundant need for a closer coupling of strategic thinking with operational decision making. As we review each of these phases, it is important to keep in mind that firms progress at different rates through the phases, depending on their circumstances.

Phase One: Budget-Based Planning

In the budget-based approach, planning is mainly a problem of extended budgeting with the emphasis on forecasts of revenues, costs, and capital needs for the coming year. If longer periods are contemplated, the budget is simply extrapolated further. Associated with the functional budgets are tactical action plans for each function. For example, the sales and distribution plan would summarize the steps to change the size and deployment of the sales force or the distributors.

The absence of formal planning does not imply a lack of strategic thinking. A straightforward functional organization, in a fairly simple and predictable market environment with management who have a thorough intuitive understanding of their situation, may have little to gain from greater formality. A good example is Lufkin Industries, which dominates the market for oil well pumps, and reported 1980 earnings of $35 million on sales of $270 million.[5] The essence of their strategy is the continuation of (1) quality standards that ensure exceptional reliability of operation, (2) a focus on market segments that require a higher level of power transmission technology than can be met by new entrants, and (3) low manufacturing cost, benefiting from volume production and vertical integration. The last element of the strategy is aided by a slow rate of change in technology—the basic pump design hasn't changed in fifty years. Lufkin is one of the few companies to produce the gearboxes it uses, which are crucial to assuring reliability and long life. Finally, no evidence exists that the company wishes to grow beyond traditional limits—hardly surprising, as earnings have more than doubled in the past four years.

Phase Two: Long-Range Planning

During the sixties and early seventies, many companies outgrew their budget-based planning systems. Implicitly understood strate-

---

5. Stuart (1981).

gies were not sufficient to direct growing organizations serving increasingly complex and segmented markets with wide ranges of products. During this period, steady growth was the dominant feature of the economic environment. In response, long-range plans were formulated to assess the financial implications of discernable current trends. While this approach to planning improved the quality of decision making by making responses to trends more timely, it was inherently limited by the assumption that the future would bring more of the past.

Organization structures were also evolving in this period, and simple functional designs were giving way to decentralized profit centers. Long-range planning per se had little direct influence on the strategic direction of these profit centers, as it was largely a corporate financial planning activity. Instead, strategic direction came from the product-market choices articulated in the marketing plan and the capital investment projects approved as part of the capital budgeting process.

Long-range plans tend to be built up from projections provided by profit centers and operating units that have access to the necessary information. One unfortunate consequence is that by the time these accumulated and detailed plans reach the top, virtually no opportunity exists for injecting fresh insight about the future. A further limitation is that the component plans, and the resulting consolidated plan, tend to be overly optimistic. This effect results primarily from the desire of those making the projections to do better in the future. This optimism tends to exist in both weak and strong parts of the organization, thereby blurring the distinctions between the two that could serve to guide the effective allocation of resources. Finally, "the plans are really more short range than anyone cares to admit. . . . Since there is so much work involved, the first year usually gets the most thorough analysis. After all, the manager knows he can make changes in following years; it is only the coming year that cannot be changed—this year becomes the budget. . . . Anyway, most rewards for performance are only measured by first year results." [6]

Phase Three: Strategic Planning

Long-range planning, based on the assumption that the future will resemble the past, was an early victim of the discontinuities of the mid-seventies. First the energy crisis occurred, with the sudden

---

6. Tregoe and Zimmerman (1980).

quadrupling of petroleum prices, followed by materials shortages, recession, and strains on working capital and balance sheets from inflation and high interest costs. Suddenly, management was preoccupied with managing a capital crunch in a slow growth environment. In response, the corporate planning orientation shifted from managing growth toward more centralized management of resources. Sorting out winning businesses from losers that were draining cash, and consolidating strong competitive positions became the primary concerns.

The dominant features of the planning systems that evolved in response to those challenges are as follows:

- The grouping of related businesses and products into strategic business units (SBUs) or organizational entities large enough and homogeneous enough to exercise control over the most strategic factors affecting their performance.

- Strategic direction is provided by strategic market plans that specify the product-market scope and focus of the SBU, the strategic thrust, and the performance objectives for the SBU within the context of the overall corporate mission and strategy.

- There is explicit consideration of distinct strategy alternatives, varying in terms of risk-reward profile or the priority assigned to different objectives, such as market share gains versus short-run profitability. Indeed, one way to determine whether a company has advanced to this phase of planning is to ask managers whether their boss would regard presenting strategy alternatives as a sign of indecisiveness.

- Objectives for different SBUs are tailored to reflect differences in their strategic position and competitive environment that will influence long-run growth and profit potential. By contrast, all business units or divisions in phase-two planning structures are assigned similar growth and profit goals, frequently in disregard of their capacity to achieve those objectives.

- The use of a portfolio logic to allocate resources in recognition of differences in the contributions of different SBUs to the achievement of corporate objectives for growth and profitability. A key is whether the SBU is designated a net cash generator or cash user.

- Capital budgeting decisions reflect both the strategic thrust of the SBU and the desirability of specific projects measured by discounted cash flow. These decisions are made within the context of the overall financial resources of the corporation and its strategic financial plan.

According to a recent survey of planning practices in diversified companies,[7] most companies have not fully advanced to a phase-three planning process. Yet, for several years, there have been pressures for progress beyond this point to cope with a new set of challenges.

Toward Strategic Management

The next stage of evolution of strategic planning practice will build on the strengths of existing strategic planning systems while overcoming the weaknesses.

The first problem is simply that the challenges of the eighties are different from those that spawned strategic planning. Most notably, competitive pressures have become even more acute as companies recognize that in a slow growth economy, they must actively seek new opportunities to grow or even to hold their position. Merely attempting to consolidate present positions is not enough. At the same time, technological advances, deregulation, high energy costs, changing demographics, a reduced government role, and innumerable other factors are presenting new challenges and new sources of competition. As a result, patterns of competition are becoming more complex, market boundaries are becoming fuzzy, and sustaining a competitive advantage is becoming increasingly difficult.

Second, recognition is growing that strategic planning systems that emphasize centralized resource allocation are unbalanced. Instead, the need is to pay greater attention to the integration of strategic plans and operational planning. Too many plans have failed from lack of commitment by operating management. A further encouragement to decentralization is that for many firms, adequate funding is available for attractive projects. While corporate-level resource allocation problems remain important, they are no longer paramount.

In response to these changes, plus uneven experience in applying strategic planning, companies are again reshaping their planning systems. Directions for change include:

1. Focusing planning processes on the search for competitive advantage. This focus assigns a much higher priority to

7. This is reported in Gluck, Kaufman, and Walleck (1980).

understanding changes in key success factors, market segment requirements, and competitors' strategies, and requires managers to specify the implications of these changes for the position of the business in the market.

2. Closer integration of operations and strategic planning. This means wider participation of operating management in the planning process to ensure that there is shared understanding of opportunities, key success factors, and implementation issues. The Caterpillar Tractor Company illustrates the payoff from a strategy that integrates the organization. From 1975 to 1979, this company recorded an average return on capital of 17.3 percent and an average revenue growth of 17.2 percent—a performance almost 50 percent better than the average Fortune 1000 company. This achievement was made through a single-minded focus on customer needs and on methods to meet them quickly. In each of their businesses—construction equipment, engines, and materials handling—management concentrates on building high-quality, reliable products and on assuring complete servicing. This strategy pervades product design decisions, manufacturing methods, and marketing strategies. For example, parts inventories are controlled to ensure forty-eight-hour delivery of any item to any customer in the world. To encourage their independent dealers to keep full stocks at all times, the company will repurchase parts or equipment the dealers cannot sell.

3. Orienting the capital budgeting system to emphasize the funding of strategies rather than discrete projects. This orientation may entail varying the hurdle rates for different businesses to reflect their strategic thrust, or setting low hurdle rates and evaluating capital appropriation requests in light of the business strategy. One senior executive described the philosophy behind this latter approach:

"No matter how high the hurdle rate is set, any good manager will be able to get the numbers to come out right. There is nothing wrong with this. It shows commitment to projects instead of numbers. We don't want managers to concentrate on rigging the numbers. We want them to concentrate on whether a specific project makes strategic sense."[8]

---

8. Bettis and Hall (1981).

4. Greater emphasis on strategic issues. The temptation is great to fit strategic planning within the annual budget cycle, whereas it should be the other way around. This attempt is often counterproductive, because strategic planning then becomes a bureaucratic, time-consuming exercise rather than an opportunity to reassess the fundamental direction of the business. Annual strategic planning is often out of phase with the implementation cycle, for it may be several years before a new strategic thrust is put in place and the results can be assessed. Annual revisions, undertaken for the sake of a mandated planning cycle, may lead to unnecessary revisions that prevent a fair test of the strategy. In recognition of these problems, many companies are scheduling major strategic reviews every two or three years. During the intervening period, the focus is on the resolution of strategic issues. These are specific developments that are likely to have an important impact on the ability of the business to meet its objectives. These developments may range from new product opportunities to potential threats from government actions or backward integration decisions by customers.

The sum total of these changes is a streamlined but more competitively focused approach to planning that endeavors to integrate the planning process with the implementation of the plans. This approach is what most commentators mean by strategic management. This perspective will pervade this book, especially in our view of strategy.

Summary

For a business to succeed in the long run, the pattern in the stream of decisions that reflects its strategy must enable the business to gain and sustain a competitive advantage.

Strategies may be developed explicitly through formal strategic planning, or may evolve implicitly through the actions and reactions of individual functional departments. Firms are increasingly adopting planned approaches that have four related elements: (1) an external orientation, (2) a sequential process for formulating strategies, which is facilitated by (3) various analysis methods, and (4) a commitment to action emerging from top-down and bottom-up dialogue. Just as strategic planning helps a business to respond effectively to changing environmental conditions, so must the planning system continually evolve in response to new circumstances. We are now in the fourth phase of evolution, having passed from budget-based planning to long-range planning to strategic planning, on the way to strategic management.

The Nature of Strategic Market Planning.   As the title implies, this book does not address the whole gamut of strategic decisions. Our focus is on the planning process that yields decisions on how a business unit can best compete in the markets it elects to serve. Strategic decisions at this level are not strategic market decisions unless they are based on assessments of product markets or pertain to the basis for advantage in the marketplace. In reality, this excludes few significant functional decisions. Even the choice of inventory control system or production process may impact the cost position or level of service, and thus enhance or detract from the competitive advantage. Indeed, few activities at the business level will serve the organization's needs unless they are externally oriented.

The strategic market plan—that is, the output of the planning process—serves as a blueprint for the deployment of the skills and resources of the business unit and specifies the short- and long-run results that are expected. In many companies, these are called strategic business plans. In our view, this term is not as effective in communicating the necessity for an external focus at this level of the organization. Regardless of the label on the plan, it is necessarily much broader than the annual marketing plan for a separate brand or product line. These latter plans deal with the precise specification of target segments and the details of the marketing mix used to reach, persuade, and service these segments. As such, they are only one of a variety of functional plans needed to support the market strategy.

The Anatomy of Competitive Strategies

The meaning of strategy was originally shaped in military settings. Strategy meant the planned deployment and use of military forces and materiel to achieve specific objectives. Effective military strategies were based on knowledge of the enemy's strength and positioning, the physical features of the battleground, and the resources available to the military commander.

Strategy: What you do to achieve your objectives.

—*Anonymous*

Business people have found it easy to use military terms to describe their situations.[1] Companies engage in price "wars," "border clashes," and "skirmishes." When Folger's entered the coffee market in the eastern United States from its "base" in the West, a "market invasion" occurred. General Foods engaged in "guerrilla warfare" to repel this "attack." A company's advertising is its "propaganda arm," its salespeople are the "shock troops," and marketing research is "intelligence."

The military analogy is most insightful when the objective of a strategy is interpreted as achieving a better state of peace rather than annihilating the competition. Businesses seek to sustain positions in markets in which they have a distinct advantage. Attacks against these stable positions occur when some competitors do a poor job of serving the market, other competitors achieve new sources of advantage, or market requirements change and new opportunities are created. Thus, a useful definition of a business strategy is *integrated actions in the pursuit of sustainable competitive advantage.*

This definition is not sufficient for our purposes, because it does not indicate how the strategy will be achieved. To improve it, we must first relax the presumption of military strategy that critical resources may not be available at any price when they are needed.

---

1. Kotler and Singh (1981).

A business with an attractive market opportunity, however, can raise cash from outside sources, borrow people from other parts of the organization, and use independent manufacturers' agents to reach new product markets. Thus, a key element in a business strategy is deciding whether the business is expected to sustain itself solely with its own resources.

Military strategy further confines our thinking about business strategy, because the underlying emphasis is on making gains at the expense of someone else. This deflects us from the theme of the marketing concept, which emphasizes the rewards from better serving customers. An effective business strategy is not a zero-sum game, where customers or distributors gain or lose at the expense or benefit of the business. Thus, explicit strategic attention must be given to the benefits the business will provide to the markets it chooses to serve.

To be useful as the basis for a course of action, a statement of strategy must at a minimum include the following elements:

- *a definition of the business* that specifies the arena in which the SBU will compete,
- *the strategic thrust* of the SBU, which describes both the investment strategy and the source of competitive advantage,
- *the supporting strategic actions* to be taken to carry out the strategic thrust, and
- *the tactical or operating programs* that outline the specific steps to be taken to implement the strategy.

The purpose of this chapter is to amplify each of these elements of an overall business unit strategy and describe how they are related. At this juncture, we are separating the means—the strategy to be employed—from the ends or the objectives to be achieved. While they are closely intertwined and must eventually be congruent, strategies must not be confused with objectives.

Defining the Business

The purpose of a business definition is to specify the present or prospective scope of an SBU's activities. The following definitions are representative of the type of statements that appear in a strategic plan:

- *Letraset Company*: Supply dry-transfer graphic designs to the commercial art market.

- *Housewares Manufacturer*: Provide consumers with functional aids to increase the enjoyment or psychic fulfillment of selected life-styles, including personal care, preparation of food, and care of personal surroundings.

- *Hooker Chemical Company*: Provide and maintain metal finishing systems for the automotive industry.

- *VISA Services*: Enable customers to exchange value—to exchange virtually any asset, including cash on deposit, the cash value of life insurance or the equity in a home, for virtually anything anywhere in the world.

What have we learned from each of these business definitions? First, they direct attention to the true function of the business. This requires an explicit recognition of the ways the business satisfies the needs of its target customers. Thus, the Hooker Chemical definition is more meaningful than simply saying, "we are in the business of selling chemicals for plating." Nonetheless, a frequent mistake is to define a business only in terms of the characteristics of the products or services that are sold.

Second, business definitions establish the boundaries of business effort and the horizons for growth. Letraset could have been defined more broadly as meeting the needs of commercial artists for convenient methods of creating graphic designs. This broader definition subsumes the previous one and implies significant activity beyond the dry-transfer product line. Whether such a broadening is desirable is a strategic question.

Finally, the business definition provides a basis for detailed strategy analysis. It specifies the first level of market segmentation that allows strategic differentiation. Comparisons with competitors are also facilitated. For example, the Snap-On Tool Company defines the scope of its business as hand tools for the professional mechanic. This market is reached solely through direct sales at the work location: factory, garage, machine shop, and so forth. Most of the competitors, such as Sears, Roebuck, define their scope more broadly to encompass many other customer segments.

Although the business definition is the starting point for the strategic planning process, the outcome of the process is often a redefinition of the business. Thus, a "chicken and egg" relationship exists with the other elements of strategy. For example, a large lumber company in the business of selling standard dimension lumber and plywood through wholesale lumber yards was forced to reassess its strategy because of the increasing importance of large-scale tract builders. This segment purchased directly from manufacturers and required drop shipments to the job site. The dilemma for the company was that if they went direct, they would be cut off by the lumber yards, who would go elsewhere for their lumber supply. Nonetheless, in full recognition of this consequence, they redefined their business as "the provision of prepacked building components to large-scale builders." This change had implications for every element of their strategy. For example, a substantial upgrading of manufacturing facilities was required so they could mass-produce door and window frames, beams, and so forth to achieve a cost advantage in competitive bidding situations. Thus, the business definition influences, and is influenced by, other strategic decisions.

Multidimensional Business Definition

The scope of a business is defined by the choices along each of the following dimensions.[2]

Customer functions. The dimension of customer functions addresses the benefits being provided. We start here on the grounds that customers seek benefits from products or services rather than the products or services themselves. The usage situation or application that the customer contemplates dictates the benefits being sought. The manufacturer then provides a package of functions, which may incorporate auxiliary services and other enhancements, to deliver these benefits. For example, adjustable speed-control devices provide a speed-control function, and pasta products may be used as nonvegetable meat supplements.

The classic problem for a business is the choice between a broad definition, representing a generic function, and a narrow subfunction. The hierarchical relationship of functions complicates this problem. At the top of the hierarchy is a generic function such as transportation, nutrition, or speed control. However, each generic function can be subdivided endlessly. The speed-control function can be divided, for example, by size of input power source (greater or less than 100 HP motors), harshness of operating environments (toxic, abrasive, dusty, etc.), precision of control, and so forth. As functions become more narrowly defined, they usually correspond

2. This approach to business definition was first suggested by Abell (1980).

more closely to the specific benefits that a distinct customer segment seeks.

Technology dimension. Technologies are the alternative ways a particular function can be performed. Several different technologies may provide the same function or satisfy the same needs. For example, the generic medical diagnosis function can be serviced by X ray, computerized tomography, and infrared and ultrasound technologies. A business can elect to employ all technologies, any single technology, or any combination of technologies. A major consideration in the choice of number of technologies is present or potential direct competitors. This question is usually resolved at the subfunction level. Two technologies may often compete for some of the same functions, but in some specialized subfunctions, only one technology can feasibly perform. This is potentially a protected niche for a narrowly defined company.

Customer segment dimension. A customer segment is a group of customers seeking similar benefits and sharing characteristics that are strategically relevant. The extent to which a business participates in one or more customer segments depends first on the significance of the differences in the behavior between segments. The second question is the extent to which the segment groups can readily be identified using such familiar variables as user industry, size, demography, or buying behavior. The choice of target segments will then depend on resources available, potential for product differentiation, and the positions of competitors.

Geography is one of the most important factors in the choice of customer scope. Many companies limit their scope to regional or national markets because of freight costs, delivery time, or perishability considerations. Beyond national boundaries, tariffs and other barriers to international trade may lead to constraints on geographic scope.

Stages in the value-added system. The final dimension is the choice of where to participate in the sequence of stages from raw materials to completed products. Producers of raw materials such as metals and basic chemicals, or producers of intermediate components such as plastics and semiconductors, may sell only to "downstream" customers or may integrate forward to produce the finished products. Electronics companies such as Texas Instruments, which sells calculators to retail channels, have employed the latter approach. A significant trend in the office products business, notably among minicomputer and copier manufacturers, is the forward definition of their business scope to incorporate company-operated retail outlets.

Advantages of the Multidimensional Approach

A display of the scope of the business—along three of the four most relevant dimensions—is a valuable aid to strategic thinking. First, it helps communicate the current and prospective definitions of the businesses. Second, it forces managers away from potentially myopic product orientation and toward the broader perspective of customer benefits and functions. For example, the three-dimensional portrayal of the evolution of the business definition of Federal Express yields several insights.[3] The company originally entered the business of overnight delivery of small packages from one place to another with a fleet of their own planes. Their competition consisted of airfreight forwarders that collected freight of any size and sent it by scheduled airline, and trucking companies that serviced city pairs within overnight driving distance. Federal Express recently broadened their business definition to include "extremely urgent" overnight letters. Plans have already been announced to further expand the business by employing new technologies and serving new geographic markets. As Figure 2.1 shows, they plan to electronically transmit facsimile copies delivered to and from their drop-off centers. This plan adds a new, same-day delivery function to the present overnight delivery. A further logical expansion of the business definition is to offer overnight delivery service to selected countries, beginning with Europe.

The multidimensional display is also useful for thinking about competitors, especially in evaluating the degree of overlap with competitors.[4] Firms that seem to be competitors are often not directly comparable, as they have made different choices along the

---

3. The source for this analysis is Levine (1981) and Colvin (1981).

4. UPS has recently entered the small package delivery market by utilizing their collection system of drivers making regular calls on more than 500,000 shippers each day (*Business Week*, 6 September 1982). As UPS vans are not radio-equipped, however, a shipper cannot arrange a pickup on any given afternoon unless a call was made the day before or the driver was coming anyway. While this is an advantage for UPS in serving their existing heavy-volume shippers, it precludes them from serving low-volume shippers who are not able to predict a day in advance that they will have an overnight shipping requirement.

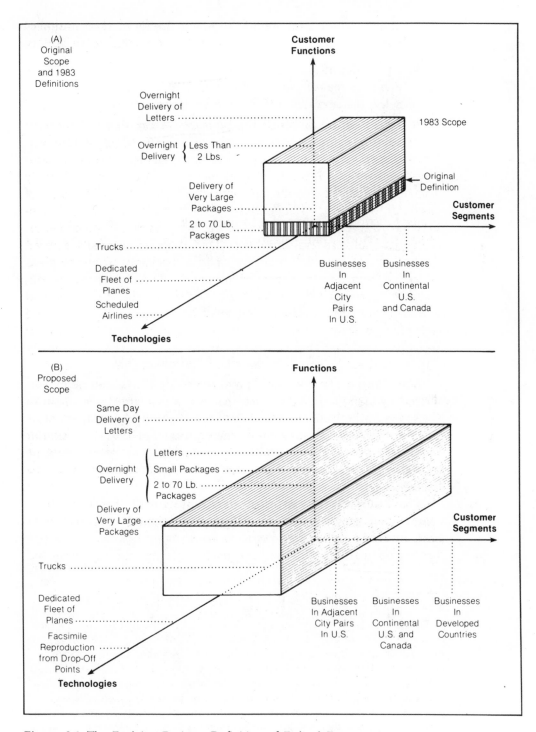

Figure 2.1 The Evolving Business Definition of Federal Express

dimensions.   These choices are often the result of two significant trade-offs:

- broad definition along the *customer segment* dimension usually achieves manufacturing cost advantages, but fragments the sales, distribution, and service activities.
- broad definition along the *customer function* dimension (by serving many related functions) runs the *risk* of uneconomic dispersion of technological and manufacturing resources.

Many questions remain at this stage: How are segment groups to be identified? What constitutes a meaningful difference in customer function? What are substitute technologies? How do firms make the critical trade-offs in the breadth of their definition along each dimension? These questions are primarily addressed in Chapters 3, 4, and 5. The concept of driving force however, can give some useful preliminary insights into which of the four dimensions is likely to be given the primary emphasis.

Understanding the Driving Force

According to Tregoe and Zimmerman, a business can be characterized by a single driving force that is the primary determinant of the scope of the business. In their view, the underlying momentum and prior strategic choices among new product-market expansion or acquisition opportunities can be understood only in reference to the central idea or concept that gives meaning and direction to the business.

The driving force can come from any one of the six strategic areas. Each area is an essential ingredient in the success of a business, but only one acts as a driving force: [5]

1. Products offered. A business with this driving force continues to produce products similar to those it has, but continually seeks new markets for these products, using its existing production and management resources and systems. Examples are Paccar trucks and General Electric drive systems.

---

5. Two driving forces that are not included here are size/growth and return/ profit, because they influence corporate rather than business-level choices. Two of the strategic areas have been combined. For a fuller discussion of the notion of driving force, see Tregoe and Zimmerman (1980).

Substitute

2. Market needs driven businesses continually seek alternative ways to satisfy needs of market segments they presently serve. Examples are Gillette Company and Merrill, Lynch.

3. Technology driven organizations offer only products that can apply technological capabilities and innovations. Examples are Texas Instruments and DuPont.

4. Production capability driven businesses focus on efficiency in production and emphasize utilization of production processes, systems, and equipment. Contract food packers and the Service Bureau Corporation are examples of businesses that essentially provide production services and capacity to their customers.

5. Method of distribution and sale. A business such as Avon or Book-of-the-Month Club, Inc., which is driven by its method of sale and distribution, chooses products and markets and develops capabilities that support and enhance this strategic direction.

6. Control of raw materials. A business with this driving force concentrates on the control and conservation of these resources as a means of increasing their value. Dow Chemical and Gulf Oil are examples.

The specification of a driving force is akin to asking which of the four dimensions of the business definition are of overriding importance when critical decisions are made. Thus, a products-offered driving force means that the emphasis is on the *customer* function dimension. Similarly, if the needs of the served market is the driving force, then the *customer segment* dimension has priority in management thinking. By contrast, if the driving forces are production capability, distribution method, or control of raw materials, the *stages of the value-added system* dimension is critical.

The notion of a driving force is applicable to both the corporate and the business level. Frequently, the driving force is the same at both levels and is a major facet of the corporate culture. As the environment presents new challenges, however, a company may deliberately seek to change its driving force. For example, Dun and Bradstreet has been the epitome of a product-driven company. This $1.2 billion financial information and services company dominates nearly all its markets, from credit reports to airline guides to Yellow Pages advertising. Until recently, the strategic emphasis was on finding new ways to package and sell the information they had on hand. This led to a proliferation of product lines functioning as individual profit centers or divisions. The company is now striving to become market needs driven to capitalize on the opportunities created by large-scale computer systems with on-line access to their data bases.[6] For new products to be successful, they must be cooperatively developed by two or more existing product groups in light of the needs of a specific industry sector. A new product, Salesnet, illustrates the pooling of resources of their computer subsidiary plus Reuben H. Donnelly, Credit Services, and Dun's Marketing Service. Salesnet is a marketing system that provides telephone salespeople with computer terminals that furnish a prospect's name, number, and a preprogrammed sales script. The operator feeds the terminal the prospect's comments as the conversation continues, and the proper response flashes on the terminal's screen. One consequence of this and related products is the emergence of a separate division in the business of providing products to support the retail industry's marketing function. Such a business definition would clearly move the emphasis from the function dimension to the customer segment dimension.

The simplicity of the driving force concept obscures difficult problems of application. Managers are troubled by the need to select a single overriding strategic area, and management teams may disagree significantly among themselves. For example, the pension trust management division of a large financial services company had a strong record in providing their corporate clients with innovative investment vehicles for their pension funds. They were among the first to offer real estate, energy, and international mutual funds for this purpose. The success of these new vehicles was attributable to their ability to meet customers' needs for high yields during a period when stock and bond returns were slumping. This evidence was used to support the position that they were a "market needs" driven organization. These new investment vehicles were offered through the existing delivery and management system, however, achieved the same purposes as the previous services, and were marketed the same way; that is, they were variations on the same theme. Very little effort was devoted to analyzing customer problems and emerging needs or developing and testing new service concepts. This pattern is indicative of a "products-offered" driving force. In this context, ability to satisfy market needs is a necessary element to strategic success, but does not dictate critical management choices.

---

6. *Business Week* (16 November 1981).

Another prevalent first reaction is that the business is profit/ return driven because this is the basis for evaluating performance. Only when profit/return is the primary determinant of the choice of future products and markets, however, can it be said to serve as a driving force. The identification of one strategic area as a driving force does not preclude the need to perform effectively in the other strategic areas.

Strategic Thrust

The thrust of a strategy describes how a business will compete within the boundaries of the business definition. To be useful in guiding subsequent decisions about supporting strategy elements and functional programs, it must specify:

- the basis for sustainable competitive advantage and
- the investment strategy, or financial mission, which indicates the requirements for funds and the purpose for their allocation.

Neither of these elements of the strategic thrust is static. They serve to give management a clear sense of the direction in which they should try to move the business unit. Although we will treat them separately for the moment, they are highly interrelated, for a decision about one invariably affects the other.

The Nature of Competitive Advantage

Few explanations of the concept of competitive advantage are more succinct—or more compelling—than that given by Marcus Sieff of Marks and Spencer, arguably the most successful British department store chain. Sieff responded to a query as to why Marks and Spencer had not followed the successful actions of Sears, Roebuck in selling insurance in their stores:

> We of course study Sears operations, just as they study ours, and we have seriously considered mounting a similar insurance business . . . .. But our research convinced us that we could not do a better job than our best English insurance companies are now doing. And, as you know, we believe that in the long run the company's interests are best served if we only do for our customers what we can do better than others.[7]

---

7. Quoted in Keller (1983), p. 148.

Businesses frequently find it difficult to assess their competitive advantages, for it requires answering three difficult questions: What is the basis of the present advantages? How valuable are these advantages? Can these advantages be sustained? For clarity of thinking about these questions, it is essential to distinguish positions of advantage from the sources of advantage and the profitability consequences.

The outward evidence of competitive advantage is positional superiority, based on some combination of differentiation, cost superiority, or operating in a protected niche. These positional advantages are analogous to "barriers to entry" in economics, but apply to the individual firm rather than to the industry. A strong position, however, is based on the deployment of superior resources and the utilization of superior skills, as shown in Figure 2.2. The size of the advantage relative to the marginal but viable competitor will determine the long-run profitability performance. At worst, when no differentiation is available to justify price premiums, and most competitors have equal costs, the returns of each competitor may be depressed to levels sufficient only to fund capacity additions to meet market growth requirements.[8]

Achieving Positional Advantage

The first type of advantage is a superior *delivered cost position*, primarily associated with size or scale of operation and tight cost and

Figure 2.2 Sources and Consequences of Competitive Advantage

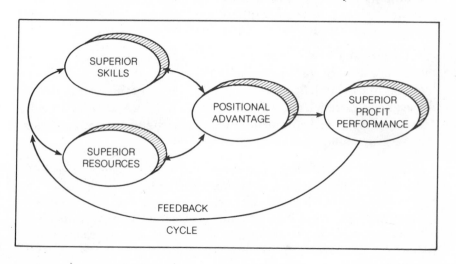

8. See Lockridge (1981), Rumelt (1980), and South (1981) for related views on this concept.

overhead control. As scale increases, most businesses are able to reduce both average and marginal costs by spreading overheads, using more efficient technologies, and gaining experience. Cost advantages are also obtainable through sourcing parts from low wage areas such as Taiwan and Singapore, achieving parts commonality and concentrating product lines into fewer models.

The most direct approach to a low cost position is to simply remove all the frills and extra services from the product offering. This is the position of warehouse furniture stores, legal services clinics, grocery stores selling bulk goods from crates in low-cost locations and airlines such as Peoples Express. The resulting lower costs are often difficult for competitors to match, for they cannot easily stop offering services to which their customers have become accustomed and are often built directly into their facilities.

Achieving the lowest delivered cost position requires unremitting management dedication to cost cutting. One of the most effective pursuers of this position is Emerson Electric, a highly profitable (with return on equity of 19 percent in 1982) manufacturer of industrial products such as appliance and pump motors, heating elements, and chain drives. In 1982 alone, the productivity of the largely nonunion work force increased by 5.2 percent. This position is sustained with heavy investments in automation and evolutionary product redesigns. Until recently, emphasis on completely new products was limited. During a period of rapid technological change, however, sole reliance on this position is risky, and the balance is now shifting toward differentiation by exploiting electronic technologies.[9]

A *differentiated offering* is the second positional advantage. A myriad of ways are available to favorably distinguish a business or its products in the eyes of its customers or end users:

- creating a unique product or service that is perceived by customers and distributors as clearly superior in value for the price.

- providing a superior service or technical assistance capability, through speed, responsiveness to orders, or ability to solve customer problems.

- utilizing a strong brand name. (Such famous names as Sara Lee, Kraft, and Kellogg are advantageous both in securing

9. "Emerson Electric: High Profits from Low Tech," *Business Week* (4 April 1983), pp. 58–62.

distribution and in obtaining trial purchases of new products.) Ideally, the brand name should symbolize an important attribute or competence, such as the association of Mercedes Benz with luxury and quality.

- providing superior product quality that in turn enhances customer loyalty and lowers customer sensitivity to price. Kodak has long dominated the photographic film market by consistently leading the industry in quality in a market in which the results of poor quality are obvious.

- being a full-line producer in a market with heavy trade-up or system-buying behavior. This is a notable feature of the stereo component market and accounts for some of the strength of companies like Pioneer and Panasonic in this market.

- being the first to offer innovative product features based on new technologies such as microprocessor controls.

- attaining wide distribution coverage, including areas in which few alternatives are available. Coca-Cola often benefits from this availability in international markets and in fountain accounts domestically.

Businesses typically employ several advantages to ensure maximum competitive leverage. Personal computer manufacturers are waging battle along a number of dimensions, including performance, features, company image, service, software availability and compatibility, and product line width.

Sometimes the entire strategy hinges on one basis of advantage. This is largely true of Tandem Computers, a company which offers systems that have several computers linked in tandem so, if one fails, the others will step in. This feature is highly valued by users of on-line terminals, such as airlines and banks, for whom system downtime is very undesirable. It is also a feature that is difficult for competitors to emulate at reasonable cost, so Tandem is able to charge premium prices without fear of competitors' price-cutting.

Operating in a *protected niche* is a third avenue to positional advantage. Here, the barriers to direct attack by the competition are overt and often the result of government policy. Patent protection is the most obvious example. Equally valuable positions can be staked out behind tariff or nontariff barriers that the home or host country establishes. In some industries and countries, businesses still enjoy relatively complete protection from imports and have few, if any, local competitors. The same results may also be achieved by being geographically located near key customers in an industry involving high capital and transport costs.

Determining the Value of a Competitive Advantage in the Market.   Just because differences exist between the offerings of competitors does not mean one has a meaningful advantage over the other. Differences cannot be profitably exploited unless they can be converted into

1. benefits
2. perceived by a sizable customer group,
3. which these customers value and are willing to pay for, and
4. cannot readily obtain elsewhere.

For example, customers do not seek high quality as such. They want the improved reliability, superior performance, and reduced downtime that a high-quality product will deliver. This logic applies to many competitive differences that management might view as strengths of their business, but in reality have not been converted to competitive advantages. What is needed is evidence that customers are willing to pay for the difference, which requires an external or customer perspective rather than an internal perspective.

BUSINESS STRENGTHS (INTERNAL PERSPECTIVE)		POTENTIAL CUSTOMERS BENEFITS THAT CAN BE CONVERTED TO A COMPETITIVE ADVANTAGE
Innovative features	→	Performance advantage, lower operating costs
Broad distribution	→	Immediate service, reduced downtime, personal relationships
Lower costs and prices	→	Greater value
Broad product line	→	One-stop shopping, fewer suppliers
Strong technical service	→	Problem solving, free consulting

The willingness of customers to pay a premium for an advantage constitutes a consumer "franchise" that can be treated like an asset with financial value, because it can be converted into long-run profits. Pennzoil has been able to hold a 20 percent share of lube oil sales through service stations and mass merchandisers, even though their brand sells for at least thirty cents a quart more than private label brands. Pennzoil, however, has a negligible share of market for lube oil for commercial fleets. The brand image matters little to highly cost-conscious fleet owners. Similar franchises can be developed with the distribution channel and converted into asset values. Whirlpool Corporation, the number two manufacturer of major home appliances, has a computerized distribution system that gives it a distinct advantage with distributors. These distributors can dial directly into the computer from a dealer's showroom for information about current stock, production, and shipping dates. The order may be placed directly and shipped straight to the retailer, thus bypassing the distributor's warehouse. This saves time, money from inventory charges, and damage from excess handling.

The Sources of Advantage

The basis for positional advantages is superiority in the supporting skills and resources.

Skills are distinctive capabilities of key personnel that truly set them apart from competition. Such capabilities could embrace

- specialized knowledge of segment needs
- customer service orientation
- design expertise
- applications experience
- trade relationships
- ability to utilize relevant technologies
- systems design capability
- fast and flexible response capability

The importance of these supporting skills cannot be underestimated. Peters and Waterman [10] make the case that the real advantages of IBM and Procter and Gamble are the decades of investment in getting their people to bring assured service and quality to their customers. As they put it, "these are the truly insuperable 'barriers to

---

10. Peters and Waterman (1982).

entry' based on people capital tied up in ironclad traditions of service, reliability and quality."

Superior resources are more tangible requirements for advantage and come in many guises. Among the possibilities are

- distribution coverage
- financial structure and access to capital
- shared experience with related businesses
- low-cost manufacturing and distribution systems
- production capacity
- ownership of raw materials sources or long-term supply contracts

Taken together, superior skills and resources represent the ability of a business to do more or do it better (or both) than the competition. The art of strategy formulation lies in putting together the best arrangements of skills and resources to enhance their combined effectiveness and to ensure that the position being staked out can be attained and defended. If the requisite capabilities cannot be acquired or developed, then management is forced to ask what position can be attained with the available skills and resources.

Crown Cork and Seal is one company that effectively rose to the challenge of finding the competitive position that was suited to their limited means. In 1957, this company was on the verge of bankruptcy as a consequence of being a weak competitor in the metal can and bottle caps/closure markets dominated by two larger competitors. As part of a survival strategy, management decided to limit their scope to two product-market segments. One was metal cans for such "hard-to-hold" products as beer and soft drinks, and the second was the emerging aerosol container market. The choice was made because Crown Cork and Seal had distinctive competencies in both metal forming and fabrication. This redefinition required the eventual abandonment of a major portion of their current sales in aluminum motor oil cans. This was not too painful, as the market was being threatened by substitution with fiber foil cans, which the company did not produce. The benefits of the resulting sharper focus were the allocation of sufficient resources to the specific needs of the customer segments to achieve a degree of dominance, and the development of a degree of specialization in meeting the needs of the target segments. This meant, for example, relocating plants to sites near the customers' plants, retraining salespeople, and redirection of R and D effort. All these efforts helped secure the competitive position from inroads by larger competitors.

Rapidly deregulating industries such as trucking, airlines, and telecommunications provide further examples of the need to mesh superior skills and resources with the desired positions to survive and prosper:

- *Least-cost producers* in these deregulating industries are typically new entrants such as money market funds, discount brokerage firms, and airlines like Peoples Express. They compete by stripping down services to narrow product lines at discounted prices. Money market funds, for example, offer no service or investment advice. The chief skill is operating capability; systems are bare bones and the organization tends to be centralized.

- *Specialists* such as Goldman Sachs (brokerage), Ryder Systems (truck leasing), investment counselors, and ROLM (telephone switching systems) offer specialized services to specific segments. These are creative, flexible organizations with superior functional support and technical knowledge. Their staff has a strong customer-tailored service orientation.

- *Full-line national distributors* such as Merrill, Lynch, Citibank, Sears, Roebuck, and Consolidated Freightways offer a complete array of services. They use a combination of automation and systems to bring costs down and to adapt products to different segments. This requires heavy initial capitalization, strong functional support for a decentralized organization, and a broad range of management skills.

Sustaining the Competitive Advantage

Whether an advantage will endure depends first on the resources, commitments, and strategies of the competitors, and the ease with which they can copy and nullify the advantage. The most protected situations are patent-protected technologies or trade barriers. At the other extreme, price advantages are short-lived in mature industries in which purchasing patterns are established and product specifications are standardized. Because allowing any disadvantage to persist for too long is seldom in the interests of competitors, the inevitable erosion must be countered by a continuous and creative search for new advantages.

Advantages also erode as customer requirements change. This is especially evident in emerging markets in which initial advantage may be gained by providing superior systems and technical service that help the customer use the unfamiliar product. When customers no longer need this help, they gain the flexibility to shop for benefits they value more, and will no longer pay a price premium. This is a characteristic of mature markets in which the search for new benefits with which to augment the product is complicated by the need to give greater priority to cost reduction programs.

Ideally, the strategic position is self-sustaining. A dominant business with superior scale and lower relative costs can take the extra returns in terms of increased profitability, or invest a portion of them in position-enhancing activities. By engaging in more R and D, being the first to invest in emerging overseas markets, and having the largest sales force or superior order-handling systems, the dominant business is able to reinvest the gains from its advantage into activities that will sustain these advantages. When a firm can utilize this positive feedback, it is very difficult to unseat. Indeed, few competitors would consider a frontal attack on such a position. This is the underlying logic of the strategy that IBM is following to reassert its position in the computer industry:

> [In 1979] a new strategy emerged: IBM would encourage customers to buy rather than rent equipment by lowering prices and raising lease rates. This would free capital, which would otherwise be tied up in leased computers, to build manufacturing capacity capable of inundating the market with new computers early in a product cycle. The flood of new products would frustrate competitors that counted on IBM's inability to deliver quickly. As IBM gained the economies that come with volume production, it could then cut prices to maintain demand and fend off rivals.
>
> IBM decided to further shorten the time needed to introduce new products by adopting flexible manufacturing techniques that make it possible to build several successive models on the same production line. Using modular assemblies IBM can launch new models at a rapid-fire pace. Gideon Gartner, a noted IBM watcher explains the competitive effect of these moves: "By accelerating the rate of product introduction, IBM puts tremendous pressure on competitors, both plug-compatible and such noncompatible producers as Honeywell and Burroughs. They must greatly increase R & D capital spending to keep up." [11]

Investment Strategies

From the competitive advantage component of the strategic thrust, we know how the business intends to compete. The invest-

---

11. Petre (1983).

ment strategy then specifies (1) the requirements for funds needed to support the strategic thrust and (2) the outcomes that are expected from the allocation of these funds.[12]

The desired strategic outcomes or goals reveal what management wishes the business to achieve in the long run. As they are aspirations, they are usually expressed in qualitative, open-ended terms. One source of these goals is the basis for competitive advantage. Thus, the goal might be to capitalize on customer perceptions of quality leadership. Usually, however, goals that are relevant for specifying an investment strategy are based on what the business wants to do with its market position and earnings. Do they want to build their position, defend it, or permit it to erode?

The funding requirements can reasonably be approximated by the extent to which investments in working capital and plant and equipment exceed the cash generated by the business from operations. In the next chapter, we will discuss in more detail how these funding requirements can be analyzed.

While many combinations of outcomes and funding requirements are possible, the choice of investment strategy is usually made from the following broad categories, arranged in descending order of need for investment funds:

a. *Invest to enter.* Here, resources are allocated to entry into a business or business segment that is new to the company. This might entail a separate unit or may be undertaken within the structure of an existing unit. When a new market is being created, the investment requirements and corresponding risks are especially large.

b. *Invest to build* $\Big\langle$ aggressively / gradually

A business or segment in this category uses resources both to grow the market and to enhance or gain a leadership position. The rate and breadth of building may be aggressive with a view to preempting competition, or may be more gradual to moderate the risk exposure.

c. *Invest to rebuild* $\Big\langle$ aggressively / gradually

This investment strategy is indicated when the goal is to reestablish a leadership position that has been allowed to

---

12. This usage of the term follows Rothschild (1976), but no consensus in the field exists. In some companies, an investment strategy is called the "financial mission," and some users call it the "strategic role" (MacMillan 1982).

erode. These "catch-up" efforts are often costly, especially if results are expected quickly.

d. *Build selectively.* In this category, the goal is still overall growth, but the investment will be highly focused in selected areas in which differential gains can most readily be obtained. The business may be expected to fund the necessary investments from current earnings.

e. *Protect current position.* This thrust implies taking aggressive steps to maintain a strong position but not to grow any faster than the market. Depending on the competitive and technological turbulence and rate of growth of the market, the investment demands may be substantial.

f. *Selectively manage for earnings.* Here, the business will limit and focus investment deployments on a few specific segments, with the priority given to maintaining and improving current earnings.

g. *Harvest.* Investments in these businesses will be limited, with emphasis on generating maximum short-term cash flows. Modest harvesting is typical of leaders in maturing and declining industries in which competitive pressures have abated or stabilized. Harvesting can be rewarding because it contributes cash and profits that can be used elsewhere. Too often, it is falsely equated with surrender, through permitting market position to erode rapidly. This does not have to be a consequence unless a conscious decision has been made to exit the industry because intense competitive pressure has eroded the competitive position.

h. *Exit/divest.* Here, management concludes that the long-run problems overwhelm any promise of profits and wishes to channel their efforts and resources elsewhere. This is normally a zero investment option, although selective investments may enhance the selling prices.

The Complete Strategy Statement

The business definition plus strategic thrust are the nucleus of a strategy. Before this nucleus can become an effective guide to action, it must be expanded to incorporate the specific supporting activities. These activities are the functional strategies, shown in Figure 2.3, that provide the essential texture and depth, and point each of the business functions in the same direction.

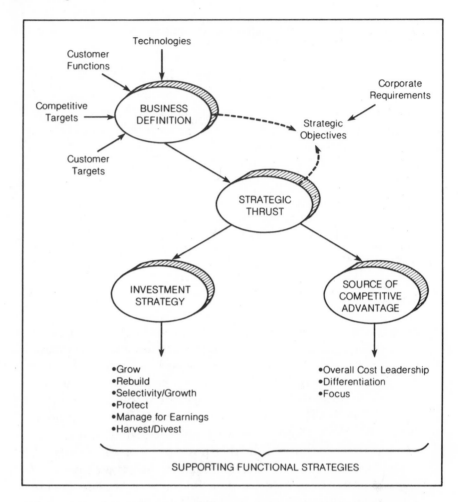

Figure 2.3
Elements of a
Market Strategy

Ultimately, as many as twenty to thirty separate elements may comprise the functional strategies. Each functional strategy has to be considered in the light of the overall strategic thrust: Is the competitive strength of the function to be maintained, or should it be de-emphasized in favor of another function? Should the function be restructured to support a higher rate of growth or expansion of the customer or geographic scope?

Functional strategies vary along the continuum of alternative investment strategies ranging from aggressively build to harvest/ divest/exit. Some of the functional strategies and their possible variations are illustrated in Table 2.1.

The principle message from the array of possibilities for functional strategies is the need for consistency and compatibility among the functions and between each function and the strategic thrust. If

Table 2.1 Alternative Functional Strategies

INVESTMENT STRATEGIES

FUNCTIONAL ELEMENTS	Invest/ Build	Selectivity/ Growth	Maintain/ Protect	Selectivity/ Manage for Earnings	Harvest/ Divest
Product Design	Lead, Differentiated				Cost Reduction
Product Line	Proliferate				Prune
Pricing	Value Oriented, Build Experience				Generate Margin
Distribution	Exclusive, Selective				Margin Oriented
Promotion/Sales	Create Demand, Capture Share				Least Cost
Service	Quick Fix, Applications				Only for Profit
Technology	Innovate				Minimum Necessary
Costs	Pursue Scale Benefits				Ruthless Cutting
Capacity	Lead Demand				Divest for Utilization
Inventory	Anticipatory				Minimum Response
Risk	Accept, Contain				Avoid

one is out of line with the others, the function responsible will then be working at cross-purposes with the other functions. Once the functional elements have been specified and checked for consistency, they can serve as the basis for the individual functional plans: marketing, operations, computer systems, finance, human resources, field service, and so forth. Thus, the business strategy provides the conceptual glue that ties these discrete plans together and gives them meaning. A more detailed example of the linkages among the key elements of a business strategy is the response of Bausch & Lomb (summarized in the following boxed insert) to a serious threat to their position as industry leader in soft contact lenses.

Summary

As strategic planning has evolved toward strategic management, the concept of a market strategy has come to mean "integrated actions in pursuit of competitive advantage". This definition also implies the important elements of a useful stategy statement.

The first element is a business definition that specifies the arena in which the business will compete. The scope of this arena is defined by choices along the dimensions of (1) functions provided

Bausch & Lomb
A Strategy for the Soft Lens Division (1981)

"When Bausch & Lomb Inc. marketed the first soft contact lens in 1971, it was the most revolutionary vision-care product introduction since the much less comfortable hard contact appeared in the late 1940s. In a few years revenues from the new lens exceeded those from all hard contacts, even though soft contacts were forbiddingly priced at $400 retail. Although Bausch enjoyed a monopoly for more than three years, the fast-growing market was soon inundated by smaller producers who grabbed a surprisingly large market share. However, an aggressive new marketing strategy has recently enabled Bausch to regain its dominance over the market.

"The renewed strength comes none too soon. The wholesale market for soft contacts has grown to nearly $200 million, and with retail prices now down to an average $150, the market is expected to triple by 1985. That prospect has lured such giant competitors as Revlon, Ciba-Geigy, Schering-Plough, Dow Corning, and Syntex. The newcomers are banking on the introduction of new types of contact lenses, and thus the real battle for the business has only begun." (*Business Week*, 17 November 1980, pp. 173–176)

From press reports and other public information, it is possible to form a fairly complete picture of the strategy that Bausch & Lomb formulated during 1980 in response to the challenges and opportunities of the soft lens market. The purpose of this illustration, however, is not to second-guess the Bausch & Lomb strategy, but to show how the known elements of the strategy fitted together to form a cohesive and effective whole.

Business Definition

Contact lenses for all types of vision correction requirements, made from flexible and gas-permeable materials, and sold to end users through eye-care practitioners in international markets.

Strategic Thrust

1. Investment strategy: aggressive investment to rebuild position.
2. Competitive advantages
   - Combination of assured inventory, consistent quality, and ease of fit of lens means faster turnover of patients by practitioners.
   - High consumer brand awareness.
   - Low-cost production of technically superior lens.
   - Special prices and vision-care programs designed to appeal to large optical chains.

Supporting Functional Strategies

Product Continue to innovate with new soft lenses that are easier to fit to different eye curvatures. Extend product line to include cleaners, lubricants, and disinfectants.

Manufacturing Special-purpose spin-casting process (to produce lenses that are one-third the cost of competitors using "lathe-turning technology"). Quality assurance program to ensure consistency of product quality.

Pricing Reduce wholesale price by 28 percent to $25 a lens to expand market and diminish competitive margins. Offer volume discounts of up to 50 percent to large optical chains.

Sales and Distribution All lenses are sold on consignment. The job of the sales force is to regularly check the lens inventory of each outlet and reorder replacements. This usually permits the practitioner to eliminate the previous requirement of two office visits by the patient to obtain a proper fitting.

Advertising National television campaign supported by cooperative advertising with local practitioners and chains to build consumer awareness.

Services Develop and provide standard vision-care program to aid practitioners in sending bills, reminding patients of appointments, and other routine office activities.

The above elements of the functional strategy were given specific attention in the published information. No doubt there were explicit strategies for R and D, human resources, and productivity improvement.

to the customer, (2) alternative technologies for performing the functions, (3) customer segments served, and (4) stages in the value-added system. These four dimensions are not equally significant to all business; the relative importance will depend on the driving force.

Second, the strategy statement must have a definite thrust to direct the pursuit of competitive advantage. This thrust describes whether the competitive advantage is to be gained by focusing the scope or by exploiting an asymmetry in the position of the business. The strategic thrust also specifies the requirements for funds and the outcomes that are expected from the allocation of these funds. This answers such questions as whether management intends to build their position, defend it, or permit it to erode.

Finally, the integration of actions is described by the choice of supporting functional strategies. These are primarily functional activities that are designed for consistency and compatibility with other activities and the strategic thrust.

A necessary precondition to a meaningful strategy statement is the structuring of the firm into self-contained business units for which discrete strategies can be developed. In practice, this is a difficult condition to achieve, for it requires balancing strategic relevance with administrative feasibility. Some of the issues encountered in defining SBUs are described in the following Appendix to this chapter.

Identifying the Focal Point for a Business Strategy: How Should the Planning Framework Be Designed?

A big presumption underlying business planning efforts is that the firm has been appropriately divided into self-contained planning units for which discrete business strategies can be developed. Indeed, the concept of strategic business units, also called natural business units or strategy centers, is one of the hallmarks of contemporary planning technology.

In practice, the designation of SBUs has been one of the most vexing aspects of the planning process. The crux of the problem is that the choice of appropriate planning units requires preliminary judgments about interrelationships of strategic issues across the firm. These initial judgments often create more problems than they solve. Stories abound of firms that initially set up 100 or 150 or more SBUs that were so small as to be meaningless from a planning viewpoint. Further problems result when the planning units cut across the existing organization structure of divisions, profit centers, and cost centers.

Ideally, an SBU should satisfy the following criteria:

1. An SBU must serve an *external* rather than an internal market. The woodlands operation of a forest product company would not be an SBU if its prime purpose was to supply pulp to the company's own converters, if it lacked the discretion as to whether to supply or not, and could not normally sell to other converters. In this case, the operation is a cost center. A gray zone exists in which the operation occasionally pursues opportunities for short-run gain or to use excess capacity. This would not be a sufficient basis for an SBU. Conversely, it would be an SBU if it could set its own prices, could refuse internal business, and had capacity to sell more than half its output to captive markets.

2. An SBU should serve distinct groups of *customers* that are different from those served by other SBUs, and should have a distinct set of external *competitors* it is trying to equal or surpass. That two proposed SBUs face the same competitors is one of the best indicators that they belong together for planning purposes.

3. The management of the SBU should have control over the key factors that determine success in their served market.

This does not mean that they cannot use shared resources such as a pooled sales force or service group, an integrated manufacturing facility, or an R and D facility. They must, however, have realistic options to use other approaches than the shared resource facility to achieve their objectives.

4. An SBU should be *strategically autonomous*. Here, the question is whether its strategy is independent of the strategies of other SBUs in the firm. Useful insights can be gained by asking whether a price change by the proposed SBU would induce a review of prices in product groups outside the SBU.

5. The *profitability* of the SBU can be measured in real income rather than in artificial dollars posted as transfer payments between divisions. This is a minimum condition to satisfy. Ideally, evaluating an SBU as an investment center should be possible, so that management can be judged on their utilization of the resources under their stewardship.

Seldom are the five criteria fully satisfied, for most SBU definitions involve compromises. These trade-offs can most readily be seen in the choice of the product-market units (PMUs) or business segments to include within an SBU. A PMU represents the narrowest combination of product function and technology and served market in which an independent "niche" competitor can be viable. It is also the lowest organizational level at which strategic planning takes place. Certainly it is desirable that SBUs contain as few PMUs or business segments as possible to encourage the development of focused competitive strategies. Such PMUs, however, often cannot be treated as strategically independent, either because they share significant resources or because disjointed and ineffective strategies would result due to excessive fragmentation.

Two approaches are possible to clarify the trade-offs to be made in forming business units.[13] The *build-up* approach proceeds by grouping PMUs according to their similarity on strategically relevant cost, demand, and technology criteria. Alternatively, one can start with a corporation or a division and follow a *divide-up* approach, using those criteria for subdivision that yield the maximum strategic discrimination. Since only one or two criteria can be used at a time, the inevitable trade-offs that have to be made between cost and demand factors are not so evident.

---

13. This section is adapted from Day (1981), Patel and Younger (1978), and Rothschild (1980).

The build-up approach was used by a manufacturer of air-conditioning equipment ranging from residential air conditioners to large commercial packages (self-contained units mounted in rooftops or slabs) to custom-engineered units for large-scale industrial cooling applications. A simplified version of this manufacturer's worksheet is shown in Figure 2.4 to illustrate how the criteria were employed. One major simplification is that the geographic dimension of the PMUs is not shown. Also, for confidentiality reasons, the details of the technology criteria are not revealed.

Whether a build-up or divide-up approach is superior in any given situation can be answered only by testing the resulting planning framework for both strategic relevance and administrative feasibility.

Figure 2.4 Criteria for Comparing PMUs

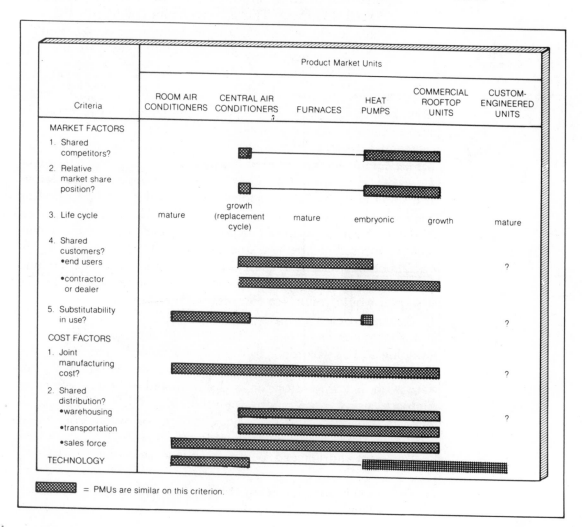

Strategic Relevance Tests.   The designation of an SBU is often a chicken-and-egg problem in the guise of the continuing question of which comes first, strategy or structure? Different strategic thrusts may dictate the inclusion of different PMUs to form the business, yet strategic planning is conducted within the established structure of business units. Some useful questions to guide the necessary judgments are:

- is the proposed planning structure capable of stimulating ideas for strategies that yield a future competitive advantage?
- is share of market an indication of relative cost or market power?
- can performance be measured in terms of profit or loss?

Figure 2.5 Strategic Planning Framework

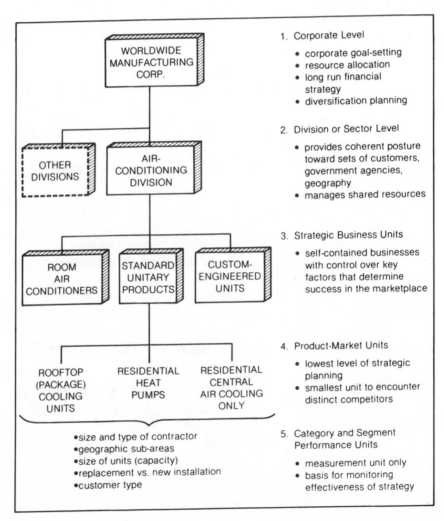

Administrative Feasibility Tests.   One set of administrative issues deals with size and span of control trade-offs. On one hand, large business units are likely to encompass shared resource units such as pooled sales forces or joint production facilities, and they can help keep the span of control manageable. If too many dissimilar PMUs are lumped together, however, program managers may be unable to perceive their contribution, and important growth opportunities may be submerged within the bulk of the established business. Further, if the business units are narrowly focused on specific product-market opportunities, the planning framework is likely to become fragmented into many small units. This places an unacceptable burden on the ability of corporate management to coordinate and control the individual units. This means, for example, that opportunities for collaboration between business units, such as adopting joint marketing programs to reach international markets, may be overlooked since no single SBU has responsibility. Finally, if a business unit is too small, it will not have the visibility or resources to warrant the development of separate strategic programs.

The second administrative issue is the extent to which the planning framework of SBUs and PMUs should be forced into compatability with the existing organization structure. If strategic realities dictate significant differences between the two structures, forcing them to be compatible for reasons of expediency may then lead to excessive emphasis on short-run performance rather than a commitment to implementing a strategy to properly position the business in the long run.

In the case of the air-conditioner manufacturer described earlier, the strategic relevance test had primacy. As a secondary consequence of the business definition, a major evaluation of the furnace product led to the conclusion that it did not fit the capabilities of the company, and therefore was sold. The strategic planning framework that finally emerged in Figure 2.5 was adopted with the understanding that the existing organization would have to be modified quickly to ensure that the desired strategic thrusts could be developed and executed.

The Strategic Market Planning Process

How are market strategies actually formulated and chosen? One view is that strategies emerge from the same decision-making process used to cope with any ill-structured problem. Descriptions of this kind of decision making have identified the basic sequential steps as: *intelligence* (search activities), *design* (develop alternatives), and *choice* (decide which alternative to select). Most formal planning process models use these three steps as their foundation.

Another view is that most strategies evolve from incremental decisions made during the constant state of experimentation and tinkering found in effective organizations. Change comes through a series of small steps that appear as remedies to discrete problems. Each increment of change is designed to be acceptable to peoples' self-interest and thus overcome the inevitable resistance to change. Supporters of this view of strategy believe incrementalism is the only sensible way to deal with complex problems, since human beings cannot see into the future, cannot grasp all the variables encountered in a major decision, and cannot imagine all the possibilities for improvement in any situation.

Strategies may also be incrementally shaped by events over which management has little control, that precipitate urgent, piecemeal, interim solutions. Responses to unexpected shortages of raw materials, strikes at a competitor's plant, or a sudden opportunity for an acquisition or joint venture may profoundly change the direction of the business.

In practice, most businesses use a combination of incremental and formal processes to conceive and change their strategic direction. A significant incremental component must be present, for no strategy can possibly be so all-embracing that every issue and event is considered. Such an effort at completeness would likely be self-defeating, for the business would surely lose an essential degree of flexibility.

There are three types of companies. Those who make things happen. Those who watch things happen. Those who wonder what happened.

—Anonymous

Incremental processes alone are not sufficient. Henderson [1] argues that because the resulting decisions are primarily intuitive and political, "Except under real stress, it is all too easy to be satisfied with superficial explanations and easy rationalisations. . . . There is no pressure to analyse deeply or re-examine the underlying fundamentals." Incrementalism also depends on bargaining. This is more easily done when times are good and resources are readily available. Bargaining over scarcity or where to retrench is much more difficult. Consequently, incrementalism with its gradualist horse trading is not well suited to periods of rapid change, multiplying sources of competition, and pervasive uncertainty.

Other reasons exist for placing initial emphasis on a formal, sequential approach to planning. First, such process models provide a systematic framework for organizing important information. The framework also provides participants in the planning process with a common vocabulary and orientation to important questions. As a consequence, it is easier to integrate the differing perspectives of the functional areas of the business. This is a great advantage, given the evidence that managers who have participated in all the judgments demanded by the common framework are more committed to the decisions. They are also better able to direct their energies toward implementation actions, because daily decisions can be placed in a larger framework.

The Strategy Formulation Process

Most planning process models [2]—including the one used as an organizing framework for this book—follow these basic steps:

1. *Business definition*—which establishes the initial scope of the planning activities.

2. *Situation assessment*—the analysis of internal and environmental factors that influence business performance.

3. *Preliminary performance objectives*—based on past performance and initial corporate expectations, with final choice of objectives constrained by what can realistically be achieved.

---

1. Henderson (1979).

2. Good illustrations are Andrews (1971) and Steiner (1979). More complex process models are described in Hofer and Schendel (1978). Further variants can be found in Gluck, Foster, and Forbis (1976), Rothschild (1976), and Vancil and Lorange (1977).

4. *Strategy development*—the identification and evaluation of strategic options, and choice of an option for implementation.

5. *Implementation*—including the specific action plans for program areas and functions, budgets, responsibilities, and timetables.

6. *Monitoring*—of performance compared with strategies and objectives.

These steps are elaborated on and linked together in Figure 3.1. Their precise sequencing in this figure is somewhat misleading; strategic decision making follows a neat, linear sequence only in such diagrams or after-the-fact journalistic descriptions of success stories. In practice, the steps are iteratively performed, with data and depth being added during each iteration.

This process model is also the basis for operational planning systems that can be adapted to most business environments. In practice, few operational systems are diagrammed precisely as in Figure 3.1, with the major difference being the complexity of the system as

Figure 3.1 Strategy Formulation Process

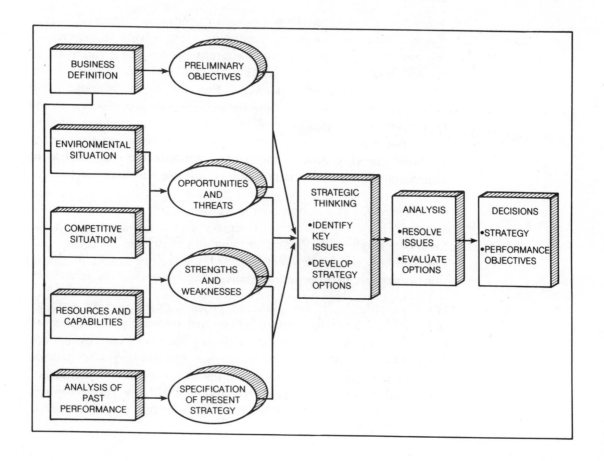

dictated by the size of the company and the complexity of the products and markets. Experience has also shown, however, that overlooking any one component—either implicitly or explicitly—will significantly reduce the effectiveness of the process.

Distinctive Features of the Process

Each of the steps, and the time sequence of linkages between steps in the planning process model, represents major areas of analysis, judgment, and decision. Nonetheless, the essence of the process can be captured with three defining features.

Situation Assessment. A comprehensive analysis of the environment, competition, and internal resources and capabilities is a necessary condition for effective planning. The outcome of this analysis is a series of explicit and hopefully testable *assumptions* about internal strengths and weaknesses, and external threats and opportunities that can be used to assess the adequacy of the present strategy and generate more attractive alternatives.

Separation of Generation From Evaluation of Options. At the heart of this planning process—and effective problem solving in general—is the notion that the generation of strategy options is a creative activity that should not be prematurely blunted with critical evaluation. There are other benefits as well. First, by explicitly looking for options, management may find alternatives that are superior to the current strategy. The discipline of formulating strategic options forces management out of a narrow, unquestioning focus on minor variations of current themes. Lastly, the effective negotiation of objectives requires that corporate-level decision makers consider an array of options with different performance results and resource requirements. Their contribution to the process will be diminished seriously if they are simply presented with a fait accompli in the form of a single package of a strategy and associated objectives that they can only accept or reject because they are not usually in a position to suggest or impose alternatives.

Objective Setting. In this planning process, objectives are both an outcome and a starting point. They are ultimately established in light of the strategic option that is chosen and the resources that are committed. At the same time, there is a separate corporate process for setting objectives, which represents the needs and desires of major stakeholders for sales, profitability, cash flow, and earnings per share performance. As these groups are not usually involved throughout the business-level strategy formulation process, their initial translation of corporate objectives into business-level objectives can be considered only tentative targets based on past performance and corporate requirements. Revisions will be negotiated as the planning process proceeds and it becomes evident that some or all of the preliminary objectives cannot be achieved with any feasible strategy.

The remainder of this chapter will be devoted to the situation assessment and objective setting aspects of the planning process. This will provide a foundation for the discussion of strategy options in following chapters.

Situation Assessment

The situation assessment is the foundation of the strategic planning process. It entails

. . . The systematic *analysis* . . .

. . . of past, present, and future *data* . . .

. . . to identify *trends, forces, and conditions* with the potential to influence the performance of the business and the choice of appropriate strategies.

The relevant data encompass both the external environment and the internal resources and capabilities. Some indication of the scope of the situation assessment can be gained from Figure 3.2, which amplifies the three major categories of analysis that must be undertaken.

Without question the situation assessment is the most time-consuming and frustrating phase of planning. First, there is usually vastly more *data*—in the form of raw, unprocessed facts, opinions, and speculations—than strategically relevant *information*. Second, much of the data are of dubious quality or out of date. Third, the data are usually incomplete in important respects, or so widely dispersed through the organization that they are virtually inaccessible. Fourth, much of the useful data comes from continuous but informal scanning by managers who view the environment from a particular perspective that reflects their interests and functional responsibilities. Thus, the major challenge of the situation assessment phase is to piece together a comprehensive picture of the prospective business environment in the face of inherent uncertainty.

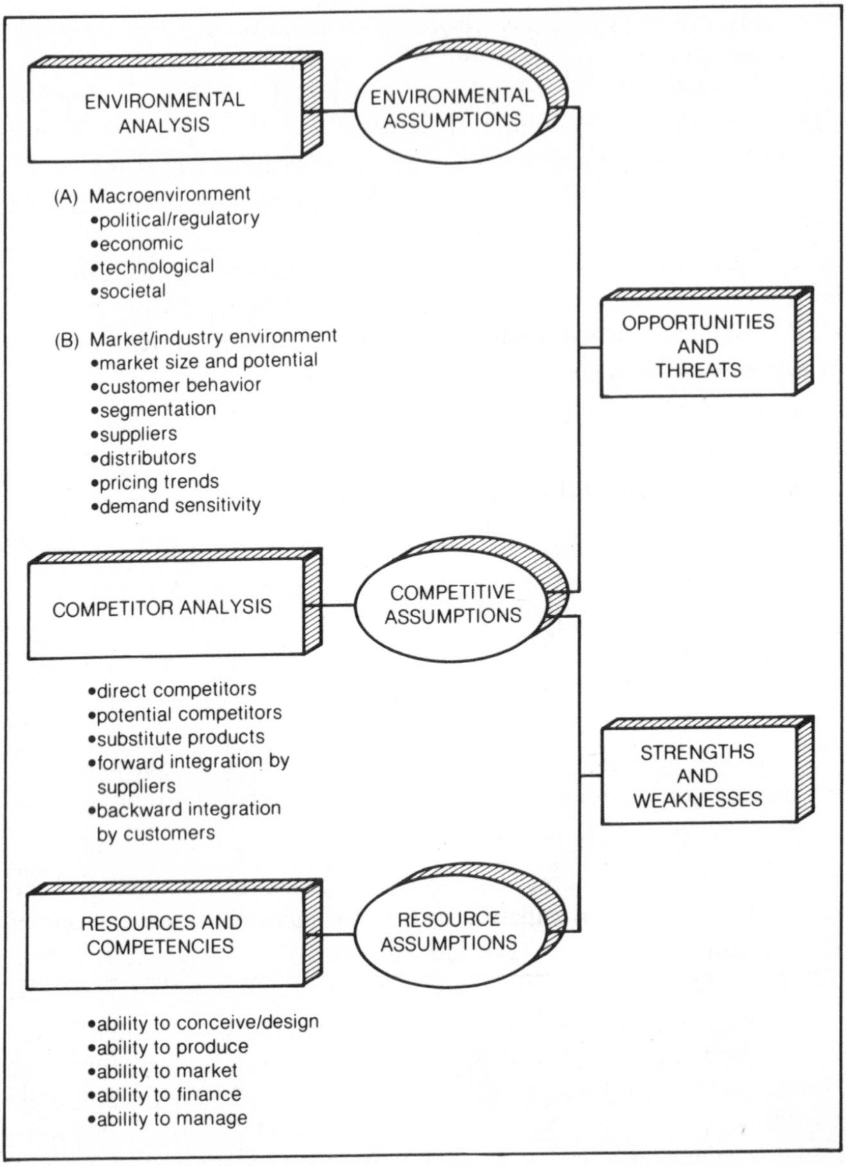

Figure 3.2 Scope of Situation Assessment

The first step is the classification of trends, forces, and conditions according to whether they represent opportunities or threats, or strengths or weaknesses. This is sometimes called WOTS UP or SWOPT analysis. This is so fundamental a form of strategic analysis that many companies start their strategic planning activities with this step.

Opportunities and Threats

External forces and conditions—whether the consequence of circumstances within the macro-environment, the markets served, or the structure and intensity of competition—can have negative, neutral, or positive impacts on current strategy and performance expectations:

Negative Impacts = Threats
- impede the implementation of a strategy
- increase the risks of the strategy
- increase the resources required to implement the current strategy
- reduce profitability and financial performance expectations

---

Positive Impacts = Opportunities
- suggest a new basis for competitive advantage
- present a possibility of improved performance of the business if pursued

---

Neutral Impact = Stabilizing or Irrelevant Forces
- support, reinforce, or strengthen the current strategic thrust
- reduce risks or improve profit expectations of current strategies

---

Because opportunities or threats are defined from the vantage point of the business one firm's threat is likely to be another firm's opportunity. For example, among the U.S. automotive manufacturers a major trend has been toward smaller, more cost-competitive cars, built to closer tolerances. One consequence has been a change from separate frames and bodies toward unitized construction that integrates the structural parts of the car into the body. For manufacturers of robots, this trend has been a bonanza, for the new assembly lines for unitized bodies can exploit the features of robots to reduce costs and ensure consistency of construction quality. For the A.O. Smith Company, which had dominated the frame market with a 40 percent share, the trend has been disastrous. The virtual demise of this market by 1983 will have eliminated a product that as recently as 1978 accounted for 40 percent of company sales and about half its product line.[3] This business is not well positioned to absorb this threat, because they seriously misread the trend in the mistaken belief that smoother riding frames could be adapted to smaller cars without a weight penalty. What this assumption overlooked was the other advantages that unitized bodies offered car manufacturers, such as lower costs and more solid cars, since separate frames are more difficult to fit properly to the rest of the car.

Testing Trends for Relevance.   Most trends are marked by significant uncertainty regarding their magnitude and timing. This puts a premium on making the assumptions about each trend very explicit. At the same time, there are usually so many possible trends to consider that scarce planning time must carefully be allocated to those few with real strategic significance. The following procedure can be used to deal with both these problems:

1. Review each of the elements in the environment (using the broad categories in Figure 3.2) and make *assumptions* about significant trends within each area. Although the trend may be uncertain, the assumption statement should be sufficiently specific to have action implications. Examples:
   - U.S. currency will weaken 20 percent against the Yen within two years.
   - The shakeout of small residential real estate brokers will continue for the next year.
   - Automotive manufacturers will convert entirely to unitized body construction within two years.

2. Make a *probability judgment* about each assumption. This will be based on the quality of data used to explain and document the trend, and the relevance of past data to the future.

3. Identify *opportunities and threats* that are likely to be a consequence of each assumption. If none can be deduced, the assumption probably lacks pertinence. Before discarding it, however, see whether it has a stabilizing effect on the current strategy, in the sense that it confirms the strategy is "in tune" with the environment.

---

3. A.O. Smith. "Safe Diversification That is Endangering Profits." *Business Week* (21 September 1981).

4. Assess the *impact* of each opportunity and threat to isolate those that are especially critical to the business. In general, high-probability and high-impact assumptions are the basis for strategy alternatives, while contingency strategies will be prepared to hedge against the consequences of critical but low-probability trends. Thus, the probability of a change in government regulation during the planning period may be low. If the enactment could have a serious impact on the business, however, it has to be considered and monitored.

An electrical switchgear manufacturer followed this procedure to identify a critical assumption as follows:

Assumption: Microelectronic costs will be lower than costs of electromechanical components, to perform similar functions, by 198X.

Probability: Virtually certain, based on trends in current costs, knowledge of the experience curve for similar electronic components, and the performance of laboratory prototypes of switchgear utilizing electronic components.

Opportunities: (1) Added electronic functions will permit differentiation. (2) Potential for long-run cost reductions will accelerate demand and rate of penetration of target segments.

Threat: Electronic component suppliers may integrate forward and become competitors while introducing pre-emptive pricing practices.

Critical Success Factors.   Another useful way to identify threats and opportunities starts with the premise that only a few areas hold the key to success in a market. The definition of *critical* lies in the certainty of poor performance if the business is deficient in the area. For example, in the uranium industry, raw materials sourcing is critical to success, whereas in the aircraft industry, one critical success factor is design capability. At any given time, the successful companies in a market are all performing well on the relevant critical success factor. Companies with large shares in the Japanese forklift industry have all adopted distribution and service networks designed specifically to reach a wide range of industries. By contrast, companies attempting to reach forklift truck customers through a distribution network primarily designed to sell trucks have been relatively unsuccessful. The problem lies in the concen-

Table 3.1 The Changing Competitive Balance in the Electronic Calculator Market (Adapted from Hedley 1976)

	MAJOR COST ELEMENTS	DOMINANT COMPETITORS
Phase 1	Semiconductors (discrete devices)	U.S. (e.g., Wang)
Phase 2	Component Assembly	Overseas (e.g., Sharp and Casio)
Phase 3	Integrated circuits (high hourly labor costs not significant)	U.S. (e.g., Texas Instruments)
Phase 4	a. Sophisticated ■ integrated circuit constitutes much of value-added	U.S. (e.g., Texas Instruments, Hewlett-Packard)
	b. Simple (four-function) ■ keyboard assembly is large part of value-added	Overseas Production
Phase 5	Assembly plus distribution	Unresolved

trated nature of the truck market, in which three customer industries account for 70 percent of sales but only a small portion of forklift truck sales.[4]

Many businesses run into trouble by assuming the critical success factors in their markets do not or will not change. Such changes present the greatest threats and opportunities. For example, in the 1960s, DuPont emphasized the development of new products and applications to dominate markets for chemicals and synthetic fibers. As the markets for these products matured and easy substitution possibilities were no longer available, however, low-cost production replaced technological prowess as the critical success factor. As a result, DuPont lost its lead in the chemical industry to Dow Chemical, which had concentrated on developing a low-cost and secure raw materials position.

In many industries, change comes slowly and does not seem to present a sufficiently immediate threat or opportunity to merit attention. With more rapid changes in technological, market, and regulatory factors, this posture is increasingly dangerous. More and more industries are changing at the kind of pace that has characterized the electronic calculator market for the past decade. This market has gone through five distinct phases, corresponding to changes in relative importance of different cost components.

---

4. Ohmae (1982).

Strengths and Weaknesses

The next question is whether the business has the resources and ability to succeed in the changing external environment. This will depend on the relative balance of *strengths*, or distinctive competences, that can be drawn on to exploit the opportunities and parry the threats, versus *weaknesses* that inhibit the ability to perform and must be overcome to avoid failure.

The assessment of resources is a difficult stage in the planning process, for its requires objectivity of judgment and consensus within the management team. Both these requirements may be subverted by myopia and are certainly complicated by differences in perceptions of what is important across management levels. One study found that senior managers tend to put more emphasis on personnel and financial attributes, whereas middle management focuses on technical and marketing attributes.[5] This study also found a pattern of unwarranted optimism at higher levels in the organization. To surmount these problems, care must be taken to ensure the context is carefully defined and there is agreement on the attributes and evaluation criteria.

What Context?   As Hofer and Schendel emphasize, "resources have no value in and of themselves. They gain value only when one specifies the ways in which they are to be used."[6] This was a major problem for a company that prided itself on the effectiveness of its expensive order-handling system. While the system was a significant strength in dealing with customers who ordered many items in small quantities, it imposed a heavy overhead charge on customers who bought relatively few items in large quantities.

Which Attributes to Evaluate?   A useful starting point is a review of the functional areas of business. At a minimum, the resource analysis should embrace the *ability to*

1. *conceive and design*, including both marketing and technological research capabilities, patents and design, and funding sources and amounts,

2. *produce*, with respect to costs, quality, productivity, capacity/readiness to serve, and flexibility of manufacturing processes,

---

5. Stevenson (1976).

6. Hofer and Schendel (1978).

3. *market*, including coverage of served market, knowledge of customers, response to customers, and influencing, servicing, and financing customers,

4. *distribute*, including cost and speed of delivery, and relationships with distributors,

5. *finance*, which considers both sources and amounts of funding, the ability of the business to generate income, and the stakeholder priorities for its disposition,

6. *manage*, including leadership, planning capabilities, depth of experience, and effectiveness of controls and measurements.

Not all these abilities will constitute significant areas of strength or weakness, in the sense that they require strategic attention. What is needed is an assessment of abilities in light of present or emerging critical success factors. This is particularly valuable during periods in which the basis for competition, or market requirements, is changing. For example, Texas Instruments has long emphasized technology as the key to its strategy. Yet, lack of marketing skills and orientation has created major problems in its consumer electronics business, and has been identified as a major factor in the demise of TI's watch business.[7] Managers tended to spend a disproportionate amount of time on manufacturing and design costs—which are critical in semiconductors and distributed computing—and insufficient time on distribution, sales support, and advertising, which assumed much greater importance in consumer markets.

What Evaluation Criteria?   Three types of criteria are typically used:

1. Historical
   - past experience
   - intracompany comparisons

2. Competitive
   - direct competition
   - indirect competition

3. Normative judgments
   - consultants' opinions
   - rules of thumb
   - management goals for future performance

---

7. "When Marketing Failed at Texas Instruments." *Business Week* (22 June 1981).

According to one study,[8] different criteria are used to judge strengths and weaknesses. Historical criteria are most often used to judge strengths, because managers are constantly searching for improvements in problem areas they have previously identified. Conversely, weaknesses tend to be judged in light of normative judgments as to what performance management would like to achieve.

Neither historical nor normative criteria directly address the basis for an effective strategy, which is the achievement of a sustainable competitive advantage. Whether the level of ability on a critical success factor is a strength or weakness depends ultimately on whether it is the basis for a competitive advantage. This requires a comparison of the competencies and strategies of competitors with the abilities of the business:

- a business strength in technical selling may be accentuated if the principal competitors rely on distributors or may be neutralized if the competitors have equally effective sales forces.

- the strength derived from a defense contract for new systems development will be accentuated if the competitor is unlikely to have access to the results of the work, or the contract is not to be opened for rebidding on subsequent production requirements.

- the problems of an aging plant will be accentuated if the competitors' strength is a new, low-cost, energy-efficient plant or location in a low-wage cost area.

- the adverse consequences of unionization for production flexibility may be insignificant if all competitors are unionized or may be damaging if they are not.

During the comparison of the business with its competitors, it is important to continually question whether the differences can be exploited through conversion into customer benefits that cannot readily be obtained elsewhere. This is the true basis for a competitive advantage.

Focusing the Situation Assessment

Toward the end of this step in the planning process, the participants are likely to feel submerged in a sea of descriptive data, prob-

---

8. Stevenson (1976).

lems, questions, and assumptions of dubious validity. It was at this point that the CEO of a major British food processor was prompted to caricature the planning process in his company as: griping → groping → grasping → (for solutions.) This can be counterproductive if the uncertainty and myriad details obscure critical problems and decisions. Too many loose ends also impede effective communication and shared understanding, for each participant in the planning team will tend to emphasize those aspects of the situation of immediate personal concern. The identification of strategic issues can help overcome this blockage to strategic thinking by ensuring that management attention is focused in the most important questions to be resolved.

Strategic Issues Analysis.   "What future cost reductions will be necessary for this business to stay effective? . . . How will the business defend domestic markets against aggressive threats by offshore competitors? . . . Which market segments might be better exploited by direct selling? . . . Do the costs of having a full product line offset the benefits when all our competitors are niche specialists?" These are strategic issues, for they identify:

- internal or external developments . . .
- that are likely to significantly influence the future performance of the business . . .
- to which the business must respond . . .
- and over which the business can expect to exert some influence.

Issues are identified by applying these screening criteria to each opportunity/threat and strength/weakness statement from the situation assessment. Some statements may have to be rephrased to be usable. Thus, "inflation" is not an issue, while "the effect of inflation on the relative cost position" is an issue. Further sorting of a preliminary list of issues may be necessary, for experience suggests that six or seven issues is the maximum manageable number for issue resolution studies and strategic development work.

A useful next step is to prepare short "briefing" papers on each major issue. The following example, adapted from the United Way, illustrates a useful format:

Issue What are the consequences of mounting competition for access to workplace solicitation?

Strategic Significance

1. Threats: Multiple campaigns at the workplace would significantly erode United Way fund-raising capacity and foster popularity contests.

2. Opportunities: United Way could capitalize on demand for access to become more inclusive and guarantee legitimacy of participants.

Potential Outcome

A. Worst case: Workplace solicitation becomes total popularity contest run by payroll departments.

B. Current path: Continued inroads are made for multiple in-plant solicitations or designation campaigns or both.

C. Best case: United Way becomes "all inclusive"; balance donor interest in selection with citizen review process.

The issue "briefing paper" also serves as the basis for an analysis plan that will clarify the possible outcomes and direct the resolution of the issue. To facilitate the analysis, it may be necessary to decompose the issue into subissues by constructing an issue tree,[9] with the top node the overall issue, such as the threat of another company entering a particular market. This issue is then decomposed into branches that refine this issue. For example, the next level of subissues might be "access to economies of scale," "capital requirements for entry," and "availability of distribution facilities." Further breakdowns might be necessary to refine these subissues. The end of each branch of the strategic issue tree represents a discrete element of the overall issue for which specific information may be gathered.

Setting Business Objectives and Goals

In early 1980, the senior management of Allied Chemical Company agreed to pursue three major objectives by 1986: (1) shift the current product mix away from a heavy emphasis on capital-intensive, cyclical commodity chemicals so at least 25 percent of pretax income would come from specialty chemicals; (2) top the industry

If you don't know where you are going, all roads will get you there.

—Anonymous

---

9. This notion was suggested by King (1981).

average for that year in both profit growth and market share; and (3) make at least one significant acquisition.[10] These broad objectives then became one basis for specific annual goals to be achieved by each SBU within Allied Chemical. Bonuses were then attached to achieving each goal as well as meeting the overall objectives at the end of five years. As a result, said one SBU manager, "I'm much clearer about where the chemical company is going."

Within Allied Chemical—and most firms with many business units—corporate strategies and objectives provide an umbrella under which SBU strategies are chosen and goals and objectives set. Thus, clear signals have been given to the specialty chemicals business to develop aggressive growth strategies. In the early stages of the planning process, however, these corporate objectives provide only preliminary guidance, for they have not yet been tailored to the reality of what can be achieved by the SBU, given its competitive situation and available resources. The purpose of this section is to introduce the process by which business goals and objectives are negotiated. First we have to clarify the differences between goals and objectives, for this is an area of considerable confusion in the planning literature.

Characteristics of
Useful Objectives and Goals [11]

Objectives are desired or needed results to be achieved by a specific time. An objective can be set for virtually any or all areas of performance of a business unit, cost center, product group, or individual within the organization. At the business level, it is common to find specific objectives relating to:

- profitability (ROS, $ profits)
- cash flow
- utilization of resources (ROI, RONA, and other measures are briefly described in the Appendix)
- market position (share)

---

10. "The Hennessy Style May be What Allied Needs," *Business Week* (11 January 1982).

11. The meanings assigned to objectives and goals in this book generally follow Rothschild (1976), Steiner (1979), and Holloway and King (1979). There is, however, no consensus either in the literature or in practice. Thus, some authors (Richards 1978) consider objectives, goals, and purposes as interchangeable terms, and others (Hofer and Schendel 1978) take goals to mean approximately what we have defined as objectives.

- growth (revenue, units)
- contributions to customers (price, quality, reliability, service)
- risk exposure (reliance on specific products, markets, or technologies)

Seldom will more than three or four objectives be dominant. The rest of the possible objectives will be assigned a lower priority or left unstated. Thus, it is useful to think of a hierarchy of objectives, representing the priorities of management.

Goals are concrete, short-term points of measurement that the business unit intends to meet in the pursuit of its objectives. Objectives and goals have a distinct hierarchical relationship. An overall objective of increasing revenue or market share to a certain level converts into specific short-run goals for each component of revenue: prices, sales of individual product categories, relative emphasis on distribution outlets or geographic areas, and so forth.

Both objectives and goals serve the same basic purposes. They provide specific *guidance* to the efforts of functions and individuals within the business. This is critical in terms of ensuring the coordination of efforts so functions are not working at cross-purposes. They provide *motivation* to individuals to perform at higher levels of efficiency and effectiveness. This is doubly true if the compensation system is linked to the achievement of objectives. Objectives and goals also provide a basis for *evaluating* and *controlling* activities. If actual performance falls short of objectives, then the control system should be able to unravel whether the variance was due to poor execution, unrealistic targets, or unexpected events. These purposes can be served only if the objectives and goals satisfy the following criteria:

1. *Feasible*. Objectives are not the product of wishful thinking. They should be challenging, but achievable in light of the strategies chosen and the resources assigned. Thus, a major task in the strategic planning process is to negotiate a reasonable fit between strategies and objectives.

   Objectives can be made more feasible by relating them to external benchmarks rather than setting absolute levels. Thus, "grow 2 percent faster than the GNP" may be a better objective than "grow at a 12 percent annual rate." Similarly, "exceed the composite of the top three competitors in return on assets" is more appropriate than the objective to "exceed the average ROI for the company."

2. *Internally consistent.* Businesses pursue multiple objectives simultaneously, but many of the possible combinations are inherently conflicting. Usually, a trade-off is to be made between emphasis on short-term profits versus long-term market share gains, or emphasis on sales from existing products versus the development of new products and markets. Inconsistency is not only likely to lead to strategic choices that are potentially self-defeating, but also the resulting short-term goals can reduce rather than build motivation. If the sales department is given a goal of expanding unit sales by 10 percent in the next year, it cannot also be expected to cut travel expenses by 20 percent.

3. *Measurable over time.* For an objective to be useful in guiding measuring performance, management should be able to tell whether the objective has been met or missed.

4. *Acceptable to management.* When managers have participated in the setting of objectives and understand the reasons they were chosen, they are more likely to be committed to achieving them. On the other hand, objectives imposed from the top down are not so likely to be achieved and may have dysfunctional effects.[12] One of the roles of an effective objective-setting process is to provide a structured basis for developing objectives that can be embraced by both corporate- and business-level managers.

The Objectives-Setting Process

The objectives-setting process provides a forum for the negotiation of feasible, acceptable, and internally consistent objectives. Essentially, it involves a reconciliation of what is desired by the stakeholders with what is possible.

Stakeholders' Expectations. From a business unit perspective, the key stakeholder is corporate management. They in turn have an array of stakeholders to satisfy, ranging from stockholders and other investors, unions, governments, and employees at all levels. Corporate management has to weigh the expectations of these groups against available resources and the total profit potential of the existing businesses to establish provisional corporate objectives.

---

12. Palesy (1980).

These are then translated into preliminary objectives for individual SBUs.

Negotiating the Objectives.   If the preliminary objectives for the SBU can readily be achieved with the current strategy and resources, then the strategy development task is considerably simplified. More likely, a gap will occur between what corporate management wants and the SBU can deliver for at least some of the objectives. The closing of this gap requires continuing negotiation, aimed at achieving one or all of the following outcomes:

- a change in the objectives, either by reducing the level of aspiration or by changing the priority assigned to each objective,
- a change in the strategy, and/or
- the assignment of more resources to productivity improvements, to achieve better performance results from the present strategy.

The key to this negotiation is an array of strategic alternatives, each with associated financial requirements, risks, and rewards. Objectives are ultimately chosen within the constraints of what is strategically possible. When objectives are firmly set at an early stage in the planning process, the alternatives are likely to be force-fitted to the objectives. This may result in the selection of an "impossible dream"—which can often turn into a nightmare.

Summary

The planning process introduced in this chapter provides management with a structure to aid them in focusing on the important questions of how to relate and adapt a business organization to its environment. The same process also serves as the road map for organizing and positioning the remaining chapters of this book.

The key to this process is the logical sequence of steps beginning with the current business definition. While this definition of the scope of the business may be changed during the course of the analysis, it serves as a starting point for the situation assessment. From this assessment come judgments about environmental threats and opportunities and internal strengths and weaknesses. Further inputs to the process come from the provisional objectives set by corporate management in light of the past performance of the business and the overall corporate strategy.

The process is highly iterative—requiring constant doubling back to earlier parts of the situation assessment as new insights about customers, competitors, and competencies are introduced, issues are clarified, and new strategic directions are contemplated. Indeed, the process is never completed, although the dictates of the calendar eventually require closure on a strategic direction. Thus, we move on to consider the formulation and evaluation of strategic options. An essential precursor, however, is a better understanding of the customer and competitive environment.

| Financial Measures
of Business Unit Performance | *Appendix* |

The following measures can be computed if balance sheet and income statement data are available at the business unit level.

Return on Sales (ROS)

ROS is computed by dividing net income (NI), before or after interest and taxes, by total revenue:

$$\text{ROS} = \frac{\text{NI(\$)}}{\text{Sales (\$)}} \times 100\%$$

One argument is that interest expenses and tax rates are outside the control of the business unit manager and should not be considered in evaluating performance. Many companies, however, do allocate interest charges on corporate debt to remind managers that invested funds are not a free resource. This understates the true cost of the capital employed, because the interest is a charge for only the debt portion of the capital.[13]

Return on Investment (ROI)

ROI has several possible measures that differ according to the basis for measuring investment:

$$\text{ROI} = \frac{\text{NI(\$)}}{\text{Total Assets}} \times 100\%$$

$$\text{RONA} = \frac{\text{NI(\$)}}{\text{Net Assets}} \times 100\%$$

$$= \frac{\text{NI(\$)}}{(\text{Total Assets} - \text{Current Liabilities})} \times 100\%$$

---

13. Reece and Cool (1978).

$$ROE = \frac{NI(\$)}{\text{Owner's Equity}} \times 100\%$$

$$= \frac{NI(\$)}{(\text{Total Assets} - \text{All Liabilities})} \times 100\%$$

The choice of an appropriate measure of an SBU manager's ability to use assets as efficiently as possible will depend on whether cash is centrally controlled or headquarters determines both credit and payment policies. If the latter applies, an argument can be made that cash receivables or payables or both should be omitted from the investment base.

Cash Flow (CF)

Cash flow differs from NI in two ways. First, it includes depreciation, as this is a bookkeeping transaction. Thus "cash flow from operations" is net income after tax plus depreciation. Taxes have to be considered here, for they are a cash cost. Second, cash flow is affected by balance sheet changes, such as additions to physical plant and equipment (P and E) and changes in working capital. An increase in inventory levels or accounts receivable is a use of cash in the same way that plant and equipment requires a cash payment.

Therefore, Cash Flow = Net Income After Tax
+
Depreciation
−
Δ P and E
−
Δ Working Capital

Here, the symbol Δ means "change in." These changes can easily be derived by comparing balance sheet entries for two consecutive periods. Specifically

Δ Working Capital = Δ cash
$\pm$
Δ inventory
$\pm$
Δ accounts receivable
$\pm$
Δ accounts payable
(and other short-term liabilities)

Sustainable Growth Rate

This is a measure of the capacity of a business to grow within the constraints of its current financial policies. The major requirement for this analysis is the construction of a balance sheet for the business unit that includes a defensible assignment of a proportion of the total corporate short-run liabilities and long-run debt. If this can be done the maximum sustainable growth rate (SGR) [14]—which reflects the ability of the business to fund the new assets needed to support increased sales—is estimated by:

$$G = \frac{P(1-d)(1+L)}{t - p(1-d)(1+L)}$$

where

p = profit margin after taxes

d = dividend payout ratio (for a business unit this is computed from the corporate overhead charge plus any dividend paid to corporate)

L = debt to equity ratio

t = ratio of assets (physical plant and equipment plus working capital) to sales.

This growth rate is expressed in nominal terms. For every 5 percent of inflation the real sustainable growth rate is reduced by approximately 2.2 percent. This is partly because depreciation charges, based on historical costs, overstate taxable income by failing to recover fully the economic value of depreciating assets. A further reason is that working capital increases that are attributable solely to inflation require financing.

The formula suggests some possible strategic actions if the actual growth rate is above the SGR or the objective for growth exceeds the SGR: (a) reduce investment intensity (by cutting inventories and/or receivables), (b) increase the debt load, (c) reduce the dividend payout or (d) obtain a new "equity" transfer of funds from corporate.

---

14. Higgins (1977).

Strategic Market Analysis and Definition

Effective strategy analysis hinges on the proper identification of the market. This market definition serves as the basis for addressing such critical questions as:

- What is the basis for the choice of the currently *served* market? Does the choice reflect the existence of significant discontinuities in the costs to serve the adjacent segments?

- What is the current and forecast *performance* within the served market? Elements of this question deal with specific areas of vulnerability to competition and ability to satisfy the evolving needs of customers within the served market.

- What are the likely threats from present *competitors* finding better ways to satisfy market needs or achieve cost advantages, or from potential competitors entering from other geographic areas or offering substitute technologies?

- What is the scope of the *business definition*? Too narrow a scope will circumscribe the search for new products or new markets that can utilize the experience base of the business unit. Too broad a scope will diffuse the limited resources of the business.

Successful market strategies segment the total market in a way that minimizes competitors' strengths while maximizing yours. The parallel in military strategy is isolating the battlefield.

—Bruce Henderson

Depending on the choice of served customer segments, and the treatment of such issues as substitute technologies, geographic boundaries, and levels of production or distribution, the defined market may be broad or comparatively narrow. This problem is well illustrated in the following insert, which describes the cooking appliance market. Often, no obvious basis exists for selecting one definition over another, although the strategic implications of this choice may be profound. To further complicate the problem, the strategist seeking to understand a particular market is pursuing a moving target. The boundaries of the market are continually

71

The Household Cooking Appliance Market

The crux of the market analysis problem is the infinite variety of ways that markets may be defined. The cooking appliance market is a good illustration of this complexity. For a manufacturer of these appliances, the question is whether the millions of household cooking appliances sold in 1984 should comprise a single market or should be divided into several markets. Certainly, many ways are possible to divide this overall market. Even though all cooking appliances perform the same basic function, numerous differences are present in:

- Specific *functions* provided: surface heating, baking, roasting, and "charcoal broiling."
- *Fuel* and *cooking technology* used: primarily gas or propane flame, electric resistance, or induction element or microwave.
- Design *type*: freestanding ranges, built-in countertop ranges and wall ovens, countertop microwave or convection ovens (or both), and combinations of microwave units with conventional ranges.
- Prices, quality, and convenience features.

Beyond these obvious product differences, there are differences in:

- Sales to building contractors for installation in new housing units versus replacement sales to existing homes. Further subdivisions exist within each of these groups.
- Private brand sales (Sears, Ward, and Penney) versus manufacturers' brand sales.
- Sales in specific geographic regions rather than in nationwide totals.

The multiplicity of ways to subdivide the overall market is reflected in the wide variety of choices of served market by the competitors. At one extreme are "full-line" manufacturers, such as General Electric, which sell virtually all types of products to all markets. Their perspective is even broader than the cooking appliance market because they sell appliances in combinations (such as stove plus refrigerator, or washer plus dryer) to building contractors. At the other extreme are "specialists" such as Jenn-Air, which produces only high-priced electric ranges with special features such as an indoor barbeque grill and special venting system.

Source: Adapted from Buzzell (1979a).

changing. As the barriers to competitive movement shift, both threats to and opportunities for protected market positions occur.

This chapter is based on a model of the dimensions of competitive markets, which provides a frame of reference for analyzing and communicating strategic market definitions. This will be especially advantageous when we review various methods for analyzing and defining markets. For convenience, these can be divided into "top-down" or industry perspectives, and "bottom-up" perspectives that look at markets from the customer's point of view. The final purpose of this chapter is to show how those two perspectives can be integrated.

Dimensions and Levels of Market Definition

The dimensions of a market are identical to those used in Chapter 2 to define the scope of the business. Indeed, for a business definition to be strategically relevant, a defensible basis must exist for identifying distinct categories along each of the following dimensions:

- the customer *function* dimension, or the related benefits being provided to satisfy the needs of customers,
- the *technological* dimension, which represents the various ways a particular function can be performed,
- the *customer segment* dimension, which describes those whose needs are being served and where they are geographically located,
- the sequence of stages of the *value-added system* along which competitors serving the market can operate.

Each combination of discrete categories along these four dimensions describes a market cell: a distinct technology providing a specific function to a discrete market segment at one stage of the value-added system. Total markets are built up from the aggregation of many related market cells. Within this total market, the various competitors choose the part of the market they will serve, the specific market segments they will emphasize, and the differentiated position they wish to stake out with their products within these segments. The various steps culminating in a market definition are shown schematically in Figure 4.1.

Hierarchical Levels of Analysis

The range of choices of market definition can be best appreciated by looking at the hierarchical structure that organizes the possible categories along each of the dimensions.

Levels of Function and Technology.   The notion of a unique product category representing a distinct combination of technology and function is an oversimplification. Instead, some degree of substitutability of one product with related products is always present. Thus, it is better to think in terms of levels in a hierarchy of prod-

Figure 4.1
Multidimensional
Market Definition

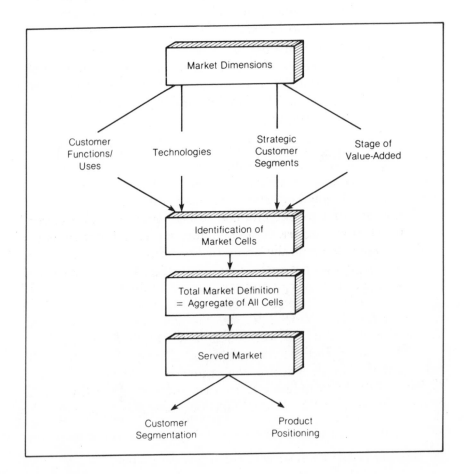

ucts within a *generic product class* representing all possible ways of satisfying a fundamental consumer need or want. The following distinctions are useful:

- Totally different *product types* or subclasses that exist to satisfy significantly different patterns of needs beyond the fundamental or generic. For example, both hot and cold cereals serve the same need for breakfast nutrition, but otherwise are different. Over the long run, product types may behave like substitutes.

- Different *product variants* are available within the same overall type, e.g., natural, nutritional, presweetened, and regular cereals. There is a high probability that some short-run substitution takes place among subsets of these variants (between natural and nutritional, for example). If there is too much substitution, then alternatives within the subset do not deserve to be distinguished.

- Different *brands* are produced within the same specific product variant. Although these brands may be subtly differentiated on many bases (color, package type, shape, texture, etc.), they are nonetheless usually direct and immediate substitutes.

Such a hierarchy may contain many or few levels, depending on the breadth and complexity of the generic need and the variety of alternatives available to satisfy it. Thus, this typology is simply a starting point for thinking about the analytical issues.

The notion of a generic product class is similar but not necessarily identical to an *industry*. The definition of an industry starts not with customers but with the group of firms producing products that are close substitutes for each other. For an industry definition to be meaningful, however, it must encompass all the forces of *extended rivalry*, including (1) threat of potential entrants, (2) pressure from substitute products that can perform the same functions for customers, (3) the bargaining power of suppliers, (4) the bargaining power of customers, and (5) rivalry among existing competitors.[1] By this definition of an industry, the argument could be made that a distinct housewares industry exists that produces a myriad of relatively low-cost, single- or dual-function convenience products for

---

1. These competitive forces are described fully in Porter (1980).

the home. However, this is broader than the generic need satisfied by an individual product type or form, as shown in Figure 4.2.

Levels of Customer Segmentation. Segments are aggregations of customers into groups in which there is homogeneity in needs, benefits sought, and response to marketing variables within segments, and significant differences between segments. Since these are matters of degree, it is useful to think of hierarchies of segments, with diminishing differences between segments in the lower branches. At the top are "strategic" customer segments, which must be served by totally different marketing strategies, in which virtually no element of the marketing program for one segment is transferable to another strategic segment. This is the reason tire manufacturers approach OEM markets and replacement markets as entirely separate businesses, appliance manufacturers have different marketing strategies for retail buyers and contract buyers such as home build-

Figure 4.2
Hierarchical Product Definitions

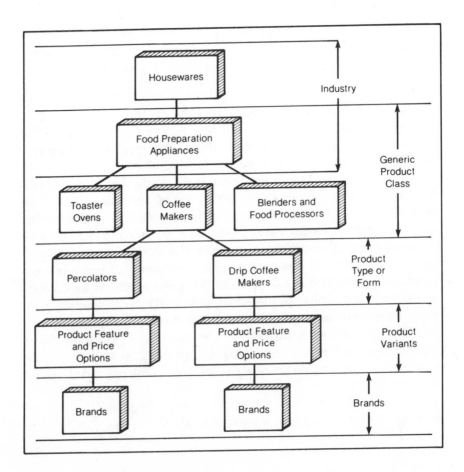

ers, and food companies often have separate divisions for institutional markets. The need for different strategies leads to totally different cost and price structures.

Within each strategic segment, further subdivisions will occur, representing more subtle differences in requirements. For example, within the bonded abrasives market, consisting of customers with requirements for selective removal of metal, wood, or other materials, significant differences are present in the benefits sought by large customers buying large orders. These customers need substantial inventory backup, fast delivery, and other specialized distribution services. Within these segments are further differences traceable to end-use requirements and geography.

Stages in the Value-Added System.   Products, and some services, move through complex stages during the transformation from raw material to an end product sold to the final user. Each stage increases the utility of its input and thus adds value. Some producers of raw materials like aluminum or basic chemicals may choose to sell only to other "downstream" producers of finished products. Others may elect to integrate either forward or backward. The choice of stages to incorporate will have a direct bearing on how the market is defined. If some competitors operate on one level and others on two, the question remains as to whether the levels can be treated separately or must be combined.

The analysis of these stages can also be useful for understanding and comparing the functional strategies of direct competitors as well as distributors and other intermediaries in the market. The focus of this analysis is on the different approaches competitors can take to the basic stages. The copier industry provides a good illustration.

Until the late seventies, the copier industry was dominated by Xerox, using a dry toner technology and customized parts manufactured in their own vertically integrated manufacturing and assembly plants. Their marketing was focused on leasing rather than outright sales, and distribution and service was through their own organization. Savin elected to enter this market with an entirely different approach focused on the low-volume segment of the market. They started with a liquid toner technology, which was cheaper to produce and resulted in a more reliable machine that was easy to service. Copy quality, however, was inferior, although acceptable for most small offices. They elected to design their machines with standard components that were interchangeable among all their machines. These were purchased from outside suppliers. Finally, they sold their machines through dealers—a much lower cost distribution system for serving the small user. Because Savin had designed the machines so dealers could service them with easily replaceable modules, they could provide fast service at low cost. In short, as we see in the flow diagram (Figure 4.3), Savin was able to differentiate from Xerox by choosing different participation strategies at every stage in the value-added system.

Total and Served Market Definition

The definition of the *total market* does not proceed one dimension at a time, but instead requires simultaneous consideration of customers, technologies, functions, and value-added stages. There is a myriad of possibilities, as the following illustrates:

■ A manufacturer of automated production equipment sells integrated systems that provide many distinct functions to one customer segment, the semiconductor industry. In contrast, a scientific instrumentation company defines its market as instruments for a single testing function sold to a distinct class of laboratories.

Figure 4.3 Stages in the Value-Added System (Adapted from presentation by Bennett 1980)

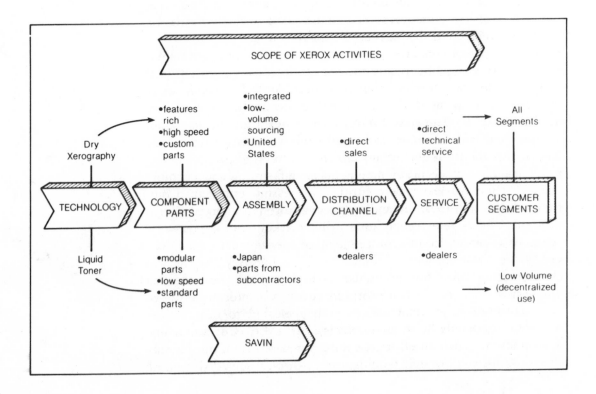

■ At one time, the market for liquid oxygen and other gases was supplied with bottled gas produced in central plants and trucked to customers. This market was redefined when small liquefaction plants could be built directly on customers' premises. The functions remained the same, but the new technology created a distinct market of large customers with captive plants.

Each of these market definitions represents a choice of how far to proceed along each of the multiple dimensions of the market. The total market can be as narrowly defined as a single *market cell*, where each cell is described by a discrete category along each dimension, or can be defined as a number of adjacent cells.

In practice, the task of grouping market cells to define a market is complicated. First, there is usually no single obvious criterion for grouping cells. Many ways may be possible to achieve the same function. Thus, boxed chocolates compete to some degree with flowers, records, and books as semicasual gifts. Do all of these products belong in the total market? To confound this problem, the available statistical and accounting data are often aggregated to a level where important distinctions between cells are completely obscured. Second, many products evolve by adding new combinations of functions and technologies. Radios have become multifunctional products that include clocks, alarms, and appearance options. To what extent do these variants dictate new market cells? Third, different competitors may choose different combinations of market cells to serve or to include in their total market definitions. In these situations, there may be few direct competitors. Instead, businesses will encounter each other in different but overlapping markets reflecting different strategies.

Within the total market, a further question is whether the business should try to serve all the market cells or should limit coverage to a subset of market cells. Perhaps they should even focus on a specific subsegment within a market cell, such as retailers with central buying offices or utilities of a certain size. The choice of *served market* will be dictated by a variety of factors including:

1. perceptions of which product function, technology, and customer segment groupings can most readily be protected and dominated,

2. internal resource limitations that force a narrow focus,

3. cumulative trial-and-error experience in reacting to opportunities and threats, and

4. distinctive competencies stemming from access to scarce resources, specialized experience, or protected markets.

Some of the common choices of served market definition along the basic market dimension are shown in Table 4.1. Each of these—taken singly or in combination—is the basis for a description of a niche position.

Market Leakage Analysis.   The differences between a total and a served market can be illuminated by isolating the specific areas of difference between a business and its competitors that contribute to a loss of sales. This essentially involves a decomposition of the total market into leakage areas in which the business is either una-

Table 4.1 Some Common Choices of Served Market

I. Breadth of Product Line
   A. Specialized in terms of product function and use
   B. Broad range of product functions, but specialized in terms of technology
   C. Broad range of related technologies and functions
   D. Broad versus narrow range of quality/price levels

II. Types of Customers
   A. Single customer segment
   B. Multiple customer segments

III. Geographic Scope
   A. Local or regional
   B. National
   C. International

IV. Stage of Value-Added System: one or more of the following
   A. Raw or semifinished materials
   B. Components
   C. Assembled products
   D. Wholesale distribution
   E. Direct to end user

ble or unwilling to compete.[2] Leakage can occur for four basic reasons, which are summarized in Figure 4.4.

1. *Functions/technologies/price ranges not offered.* Some customers may be "leaked away" because a decision has been made not to offer a product form or price range that meets the customers' needs. This is estimated by measuring the sales of competitors' product elements (including size, form, options, delivery and service capability and quality) for which the business does not offer a viable substitute from the customers' point of view.

2. *Distribution or geographic coverage gap.* This occurs when the business does not effectively distribute a competitive prod-

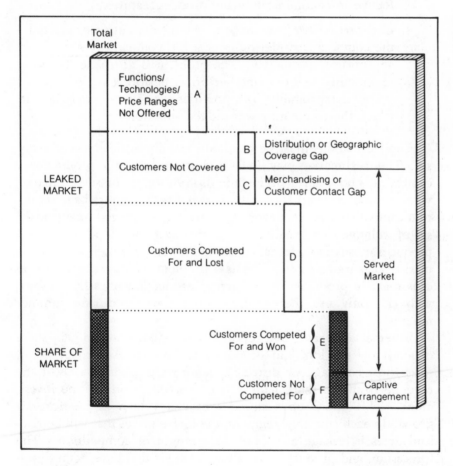

Figure 4.4 Possible Sources of Market Leakage

2. Other perspectives on this approach can be found in Ohmae (1982) and Weber (1976).

uct in all geographic areas. It may also result when a decision is made to eliminate some distribution outlets within an area, such as small variety stores, or independent wholesalers that are expensive to cover.

3. *Merchandising or customer contact gap.* Consumer product firms suffer this gap when their product line has poor representation within outlets where they have distribution. This could be due to poor locations, limited shelf space or stock on hand, or reluctant dealer cooperation. For industrial product firms, the analogous problem is having a competitive product available but finding it is not in the consideration set because key decision makers are not being reached, the calls are too infrequent, or the calls are ineffective in communicating the product features.

4. *Customers competed for and lost.* Here, the customer elected the competitor's offering after a full comparison with an appropriate alternative. The problem is to isolate the differentiating factors—whether price, performance, service, or simply compatability with previous systems or purchases—in which the competitor was judged superior.

Captive markets must be handled carefully in this type of analysis. The total market may be large, but if most of the production is captive, it is not realistic to include this portion in the served market when computing market shares. If several competitors have significant captive volume, however, this must be recognized in any analysis of relative cost position. At the extreme, if a competitor produces mostly for internal consumption, they may sell in the open market at marginal cost. This is a problem with packages such as cans that are produced on integrated production lines by brewers, who can only use their full in-house capacity during summer months.

Whether a leakage area represents an opportunity to gain share depends on the long-run economic prospects. An expansion of sales force coverage or distribution outlets is justified only if the revenue from the share gain is large enough to justify the investment. This opens up a number of issues such as the forecast growth in each customer segment, the future prices that will be realized in each leakage area, and the strength of competition. The forecasting and product life analysis methods that have been developed to deal with these issues are discussed in depth in a companion volume in this series.

Top-Down and Bottom-Up Perspectives on Market Analysis

The challenge of understanding and competing within complex and shifting market structures has spawned two complementary perspectives on the nature of markets. One takes a "top-down" and the other a "bottom-up" perspective. While they look different on the surface and employ different analysis methods, they are best used together, for neither gives a complete picture of a competitive market. The purpose of this section is to contrast these perspectives and the methods typically associated with each perspective. The next section addresses the question of integration of the two perspectives.

Contrasting Top-Down and Bottom-Up Perspectives

The top-down view is taken by corporate-level planners and managers seeking to understand the strategic posture and prospects for an SBU or cluster of SBUs. The orientation is toward the overall industry and the forces of competition within that industry. Markets are seen as arenas of profitable competition where available or attainable resources can be used to achieve a competitive advantage. These resources are usually *supply* factors such as raw materials, production processes and technologies, and the base of experience in serving that market. This perspective should also consider how economies of scale or other forms of barriers to entry to the industry are changing, or how suppliers and customers are using their bargaining power to extract concessions.

The *bottom-up* perspective is associated with operating management—especially product or market managers with the responsibility for a product-market or product line. Pervading this perspective is an emphasis on the customer. The primary task of product or market managers is to anticipate and react to shifts in the fine-grain structure of the market. These may result from changes in customers' requirements, needs, and capabilities or the ability of competitors to satisfy these requirements. This view of strategy as evolving from marketplace circumstances is different from the top-down view, which begins with supply factors. These differences are summarized and highlighted in Table 4.2.

Table 4.2 The View from the Top-Down Versus the Bottom-Up

ISSUE	TOP–DOWN VIEW	BOTTOM–UP VIEW
1. Definition of market	Markets are arenas of competition where corporate resources can profitably be employed	Markets are shifting patterns of customer requirements and needs that can be served in many ways
2. Orientation to market environment	Strengths and weaknesses relative to competition ■ cost position ■ ability to transfer experience ■ market coverage	Customer perceptions of competitive alternatives ■ match of product features and customer needs ■ positioning
3. Identification of market segments	Looks for cost discontinuities	Emphasizes similarity of buyer responses to market efforts
4. Identification of market niches to serve	Exploits new technologies, cost advantages, and competitors' weaknesses	Finds unsatisfied needs, unresolved problems, or changes in customer requirements and capabilities.
5. Time frame	2 to 5 years	1 to 3 years

Top-Down Approaches to Market Analysis

The breadth of this perspective requires consideration of a wide variety of present and prospective markets for resource allocation purposes. To implement this analysis, two requirements are paramount: (1) large amounts of data on market sizes, trends, plant capacities, and so forth must be in easily accessible form, and (2) the emphasis on resource allocation and competitive position puts a premium on the assessment of one's relative cost standing and the transferability of the experience base beyond presently served markets.

Supply-Oriented Approaches

The first implementation requirement means a reliance on published data, which are almost invariably organized by industry group. These industry groups are usually defined according to supply criteria such as similarity of manufacturing processes, raw materials, physical appearance, technology, or method of operation. The virtue of such industry groups, which are the backbone of the Standard Industrial Classification system, is their wide acceptance due to availability of data, ease of implementation, and seeming stability.

The problems are most apparent with the function and customer dimensions of markets. Two competitive products that serve the same function with different technologies are almost invariably in different SIC categories. For example, "polyvinyl" rain gutters and "sheet metal" gutters are in different three-digit categories. These two technologies may not always compete directly, but when they do, they belong to the same market. This cannot be ascertained from data based on similarity of supply factors. Similarly, customer market segments defined by industries may be inappropriate because they are either too broad (and thus obscure important differences in needs and buying patterns) or too narrow (if the differences between segments are inconsequential for strategic purposes). In short, supply criteria seldom serve as a sufficient basis for grouping customers.

Identification of Cost/Investment Discontinuities

With this approach, the analyst evaluates the market to see whether a significant discontinuity in the pattern of costs, capital requirements, and margins exists along one or more dimensions of the market. The resulting category boundaries represent barriers that insulate prices and profits from the activities of competitors outside the segments. They also discourage easy entry by potential competitors. Thus, within the boundaries, the relative profitability of competitors can meaningfully be compared. Factors contributing to these discontinuities include economies of scale, transferability of experience, and capital requirements.[3]

---

3. Porter (1979) discusses several other sources of discontinuities, including product differentiation (which limits the extent to which brand names can be utilized in adjacent markets) and lack of access to distribution channels.

A boundary is encountered when participation in an adjacent category—whether a different technology, customer group, or function—is impeded by the need to enter with a large-scale operation to avoid a cost disadvantage, the need to invest substantial financial resources for fixed facilities or working capital, or the need to employ a different marketing strategy. These barriers may not be severe if some of the company's experience base can be transferred to the new market. For example, a significant proportion of Texas Instruments' experience with semiconductor manufacturing is applicable to such related products as random access memories and handheld calculators.

Experience is not restricted to production and technology factors but reflects the accumulated output of all activities that add value to a product. For example, the costs of marketing, distribution, and service often depend on experience and present a combination of scale and knowledge factors. Whether the company's experience and related resources can be employed more broadly depends on the similarity of requirements for resources across customer segments, technologies, and functions.

Market boundaries identified in terms of cost discontinuities reveal opportunities for market niches the firm can protect from competitive inroads. Ideally, direct competition should be at a minimum within this market so the company can dominate the experience base necessary to serve that market. If the cost discontinuity is created by a cost element whose relative importance is declining, or the experience base is shared with outside suppliers of component parts or production technology who will sell to all prospective competitors, then the narrow market definition lacks enduring value.

When the market is defined broadly to incorporate competitive levels of experience and scale economies for a major cost element, it may include a number of products that are only loosely related on other criteria such as similarity of functions provided or production methods. For example, the cost position of many consumer packaged goods products is dictated by experience in sales and distribution through grocery outlets and advertising and sales promotion to mass markets, for these activities are a significant proportion of total cost. This broad perspective on market definition is useful in the consideration of new ventures. It may be inappropriate for other purposes, such as evaluating performance in a served market, since it usually embraces a number of different competitive arenas.

Bottom-Up Approaches to Market Analysis

The distinguishing feature of the bottom-up perspective is the use of judgmental or behavioral data from customers. This data can be used for the identification of market cell boundaries—also called competitive product-markets—and for revealing the fine-grained structure of customer segments and the positioning of products or brands within the product market.

Identifying Competitive Product Markets

The issue of identifying competitive product-markets has already been addressed with top-down approaches. These reveal how the economics of supply can create boundaries, but are of little value in determining which products will behave as substitutes in the market. This raises such questions as, Is Ragu Italian Cooking Sauce a spaghetti sauce or a tomato sauce? Are Handi Wipes paper towels or washrags? Are General Foods International Coffees in the hot cocoa product category or the coffee category? Do Certs belong in the candy mint or breath mint category?

A variety of customer-oriented analytical methods have been developed to deal with these questions. They can be classified by whether they rely on behavioral or on judgmental data.[4]

The best-known *behavioral* methods are based on cross-elasticities or brand-switching data. On the face of it, a cross-elasticity measure directly addresses the question of whether two products are substitutes and hence in the same competitive set. This measure is based on the proportional change in the sales of one product due to a shift in price of another product. For example, if a 10 percent reduction in the price of insulated copper cable caused a 5 percent reduction in the sales of insulated aluminum cable, the two types of cable would be considered substitutes. In practice, such studies are extremely difficult to underatake, for usually many factors contribute to changes in product sales other than price changes of substitutes.

Brand-switching measures of substitutability are widely used within such categories as food and health-care products that have

---

4. These methods are critically evaluated in Day, Shocker, and Srivastava (1979).

high repeat purchase rates. These measures are interpreted as conditional probabilities, since they describe the probability of purchasing brand A given that brand B was purchased on the last occasion. Consumers are assumed to be more likely to switch between close substitutes than between distant ones.

While behavioral measures provide the best indication as to what customers have done, they do not necessarily reveal what they might do under changed circumstances. *Judgmental* data, in the form of perceptions or preferences of product or brand alternatives, give better insights into future patterns of competition. Also, the methods for analyzing this data to identify product-market boundaries are better able to handle large numbers of potentially competitive alternatives.

Customer judgments of substitutability can be obtained simply by asking a sample of customers to indicate the degree of substitutability between all possible pairs of products or brands on a rating scale. The results of such analyses are seldom useful, for customers lack a specific context within which to make their judgments. For this reason, *substitution-in-use* techniques have been developed that give good insights into product-market boundaries. Customers are asked to judge the appropriateness or acceptability of a number of potentially competitive products for specific conditions of use. In a study of proprietary medicines, for example, respondents were asked whether each of fifty-two medicines was acceptable for a wide variety of usage situations ranging from "when you have a stuffy nose" to "when you have a fever." This approach presumes that the set of products provides a reasonable sample of the benefits being sought by the customer, and that two usage situations are similar if similar benefits are desired in both situations. If so, a market can be defined as a set of products that are judged to be appropriate within usage situations in which similar patterns of benefits are sought. For example, paint brushes and paint rollers were found to be in the same market because of significant overlap in usage, while aerosol spray paints were in a different market for specialized uses.

Behavioral or judgmental data provide only a relative degree of substitutability. Management judgment is still required to decide the degree of overlap in actual usage or perceived appropriateness that constitutes an effective level of competition. Equally important insights come from knowledge of the reasons why two products or brands behave as substitutes.

Customer Segmentation

A product-market definition carves out a distinct arena in which to compete, but gives little guidance on how to compete. For this purpose, what is needed is a segmentation of the customers for the products into groups whose members behave in the same way or have similar needs. These needs are reflected in the benefits customers seek from the "augmented" product, including information, service, technical support, and other nonproduct features of the total offering. Once customer segments have been identified, any group or combination of groups can be selected as a target to be reached with a distinct strategy.

The strategic relevance of effective customer segmentation can be seen from the experience of a manufacturer of electric motors trying to develop niche strategies for the forty-seven different industry categories within its served market.[5] The breakthrough came when it was found that customers could be grouped into four segments based on common buying characteristics. Segment A was highly price sensitive, because motors were standard items bought in large lots and represented a significant proportion of the end-product cost. This segment did their own applications engineering and cared little for features. At the other extreme was Segment D, containing small-lot buyers who manufactured specialty items. They insisted on high quality and special features, and relied on their suppliers for applications engineering. Because motors were a small portion of their total costs, and their purchase quantities were small, they were not noticeably price sensitive.

Having defined the segments as shown in Figure 4.5, the manufacturer was able to assess its current position in the market and opportunities for competitive advantage. For example, management found that to their surprise, they were doing poorly in price-sensitive Segment A. Order sizes were small and mainly comprised special orders. Although prices were 10 percent higher than competition, the premium did not offset the marketing and setup costs. As a result, the segment was unprofitable relative to the other segments. Management chose to price itself "out" of this segment by raising prices 25 percent across the board. This resulted in some loss of sales in Segment B, but had no discernible effect in Segments C and D, where the company focused its strategy.

---

5. This illustration has been adapted from Garda (1981).

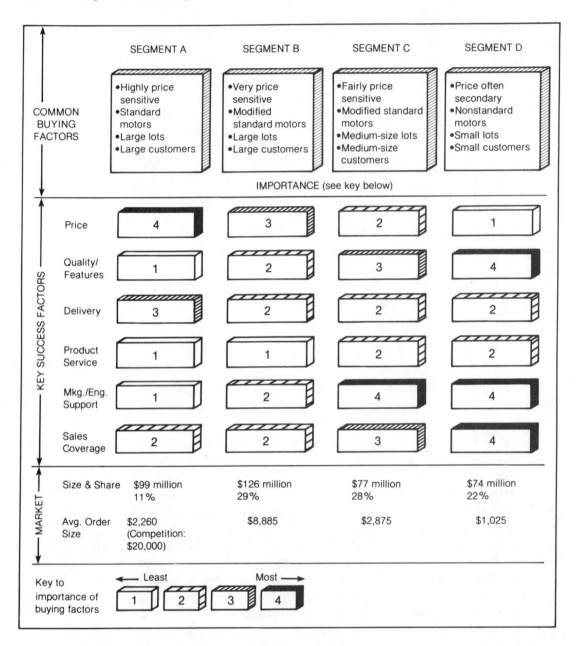

Figure 4.5 Segmentation Based on Common Buying Requirements

Actionable segmentation schemes [6] yield customer groups that are

1. *measurable* as to extent of present or potential volume requirements and rate of growth.

2. *accessible* so they can be efficiently reached and served with promotion, direct selling, and advertising.

3. sufficiently *different* with respect to needs and wants so they can justify a meaningful variation in the strategy used to serve the segment.

4. *substantial* enough to justify the incremental costs of a tailored strategy, including differentiated products, marketing programs, and services.

5. *durable*. During the introductory state of the product life cycle, there may be a distinct group of "early adopters" who are highly interested in the new product before most potential users are even aware of the product. Later, the distinction between early and late adopters diminishes and may eventually disappear.

The process of segmentation usually begins with the identification of a *basis for segmentation*—a product-specific factor that reflects differences in customer requirements and responsiveness to marketing variables. Possibilities include customers' product purchase patterns, product usage, benefits sought, price and technical service sensitivity, intentions to buy, and brand preference and loyalty. The choice will largely be dictated by the decisions to be made.

Segment descriptors are then chosen, based on their ability to identify segments, to account for variance in the segmentation basis, and to suggest competitive strategy implications. These descriptors must carefully be tailored to the context. A manufacturer of mining equipment found that the value-in-use of this equipment (which depends on the initial and operating costs as well as productivity improvements) relative to the competition depends less on the commodity being mined than on the specific physical profile of the mine.[7] Similarly, the geographic location of the mine affects its fixed cost structure and the comparative operating costs and productivity per unit of output for different types of equipment.

---

6. See Kotler (1980), Buzzell (1979a), and Wind (1978) for further discussion of the process of segmentation.

7. Johnson (1978).

Table 4.3 Customer Characteristics Commonly Used to Describe Customer Segments

A. In Both Industrial and Consumer Markets
   1. Usage situation
   2. Benefits sought or derived from product
   3. Volume and frequency of purchase
   4. Past purchasing or switching behavior
   5. Method of purchase—where and how purchases are made
   6. Geographic location
   7. Responsiveness to marketing variables (price sensitivity, etc.)

B. Primarily in Industrial Markets
   1. SIC industry group
   2. Size of organization (number of employees, sales volume)
   3. Service requirements
   4. Average transaction amount
   5. Profit margin
   6. Decision processes (number of decision makers, speed of decision making)

C. Primarily in Consumer Markets
   1. Demographic factors (age, stage of family life cycle, sex, race, religion, family size)
   2. Socioeconomic factors (income, occupation, education, social class)
   3. Psychological characteristics (activities, interests, opinions, and life-styles)
   4. Media habits
   5. Attitudes toward product category

The number of possible segment descriptions is virtually limitless, and almost every one of them has been used at one time. Some of the more useful ones are shown in Table 4.3.

Positioning Analysis

Positioning refers to the customer's perceptions of the place a product or brand occupies in given market segments. In some markets, a position is achieved by associating the benefits of the brand with the needs or life-style of a customer group (as Brim decaffeinated coffee appeals to the concerned coffee-drinker segment with the theme "You can drink as much as you used to"). More often, positioning involves the differentiation of the company's offering from the competition by making or implying a comparison in terms of specific attributes such as price or performance features. Thus, the QYX line of computerized typewriters was introduced with a price range of $1,400 to $7,750, which corresponded to a gap in the IBM product line.

A variety of mapping techniques has been developed to represent these perceptions of product positions. They typically start with customer judgments of similarity and preference toward the brands, products, or organizations within one or more market cells. The essential ingredients of a typical map can be seen in Figure 4.6, which shows the perceptions of banks in a major urban market among retail bank customers.

The dimensions of "personalism" and "aggressiveness" correspond to the characteristics that customers used to differentiate among competing banks. The degree to which one bank competes with another is represented by their closeness in the perceptual space (this assumes that they are in the same geographical vicinity). Other factors being equal, customers will then pick the bank that comes closest to their preferred combination of aggressiveness and personalism. The objective of a positioning strategy in this market

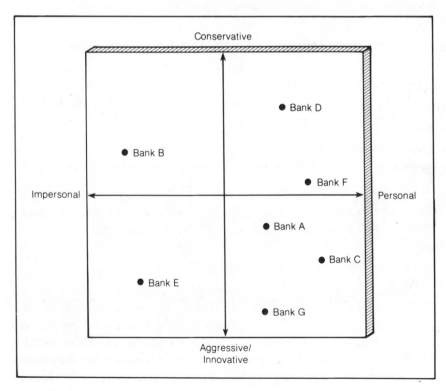

Figure 4.6 Perceptual Map of Retail Banks (Adapted from Heenan and Addleman 1976)

is to ensure that the bank is perceived as being one of the best at meeting the needs of a large and growing group of customers. Thus, positioning studies are most useful when conducted in conjunction with a segmentation analysis.[8]

Assessing Positioning with Segment Share Analysis.   Direct and powerful insights into whether a business is effectively positioned through a clear differentiation of its products or brands come from the variability of market shares across the discrete segments that make up the served market.[9]

The basic premise is that a brand with the same share in every market segment in which it competes is not positioned. A brand that is poorly positioned lacks significant appeal to the particular needs of a discrete segment and consequently is likely to be price sensitive. Conversely, a brand with considerable variability of shares across end-use segments or customer groups is sharply positioned to satisfy a distinct pattern of needs in one or two segments. Such a brand will also be more profitable because it will face a lower demand elasticity that can be converted into higher relative prices. Further incremental profits will come from marketing efficiencies due to higher repeat purchase rates and customer loyalty. These relationships are shown in the data for one brand with a distinct position in a large consumer food product category.

	MARKET SEGMENTS		
	Ingredient-Use Segment	Flavor-Oriented Segment	Nutritionally Oriented Segment
Total Market ($ million)	$600	$300	$100
Brand Share	8%	12%	20%
Share of Sales from Brand Switchers	37%	33%	27%
Price Elasticity Index	10.0	7.5	4.5

8. The preferences of a distinct segment can be represented as "ideal" points superimposed on a perceptual map.

9. Moran (1981).

An important issue is the choice of an appropriate basis for identifying market segments. As a rule of thumb, the ratio of the highest to the lowest shares across the separate consumption markets for various brands should range between 4 to 1 and 10 to 1. If all the brand shares are uniform across the consumption markets, the basis for segmentation is not likely to be relevant.

Integrating the Top-Down and Bottom-Up Perspectives

These two perspectives yield different but complementary insights into the boundaries and structure of markets that need to be integrated to give a complete picture of the market environment. This does not mean they have to be fully reconciled, for we are not looking for a single answer to a complex set of questions.

Much integration can be achieved simply through effective dialogue between corporate and product-market management levels. The kinds of planning systems discussed in Chapter 8 are one way to encourage this top-down and bottom-up dialogue. This section discusses two approaches to the analysis of markets that further integrate the two perspectives. The first approach is strategic groups analysis. The second is the choice of different market definitions—and resulting market shares—for different strategic purposes. Both are limited to the extent that they are static portrayals, and thus should be integrated with analyses of product life cycles and industry evolution.

Strategic Groups Analysis

Within an industry, some firms persistently outperform others. IBM has consistently had a rate of return on invested capital exceeding that of other mainframe computer manufacturers. The objective of strategic groups analysis is to characterize the differences in strategies among competitors that account for these differences in performance. There are three related elements to the overall concept.

First, within an industry, the competing firms have at some time made choices with respect to every element of their strategy, including scope, strategic thrust, and the elements of their supporting functional strategies. Some of the significant strategic choices relate to degree of specialization, emphasis on branding, level of channel participation, technological leadership, product quality, degree of vertical integration, extent of provision of services, and relative price position. These are the strategic dimensions that Savin explored when it sought to differentiate its strategy from Xerox.

Second, only a few distinctive patterns or groupings of strategic choices are usually present within an industry. Seldom do all the competitors follow the same strategy—nor do they all follow different strategies. Thus, within the major appliance industry there are four strategic groups: (1) full-line national brand manufacturers, (2) part-line national brand manufacturers, (3) private-brand producers, and (4) retailers.[10]

Third, strategic groups are stable and defensible because of mobility barriers that act as deterrents to shifts from one strategic group to another. Firms outside a strategic group cannot readily imitate the strategy adopted by another group without substantial costs, significant elapsed time, uncertainty about the outcome of the change in strategy, or a combination of these.

Competitive Mapping.   The strategic group concept can be used to develop a map of the position of competitors along the key strategic dimensions. For example, Figure 4.7 shows an illustrative map of the U.S. chain saw market, circa 1978.[11] The effectiveness of this mapping technique lies in the correct choice of dimensions. This is a problem, for most analyses have been ad hoc exercises that yield reasonable dimensions but do not preclude others. What is needed is a better understanding of the influence of mobility barriers as the defining characteristics of strategic groups.

The strategic group concept serves as an intermediate stage of analysis between the supply-oriented industry perspective and demand-oriented factors that influence the segmentation structure of the market. Indeed, many of the mobility barriers are a consequence of market variables that can be best studied from a customer perspective.

Multiple Market Shares

No other nonfinancial measure of the position of a business is as widely used—and useful—as market share. Because it is the most direct indicator of the relative competitive position of a business, it has exceptional diagnostic value. Frequently, it is a major determinant of profitability. For these reasons, it is an important business objective to be pursued in its own right, as well as a determinant of other desirable objectives.

---

10. Hunt (1972).
11. Porter (1980).

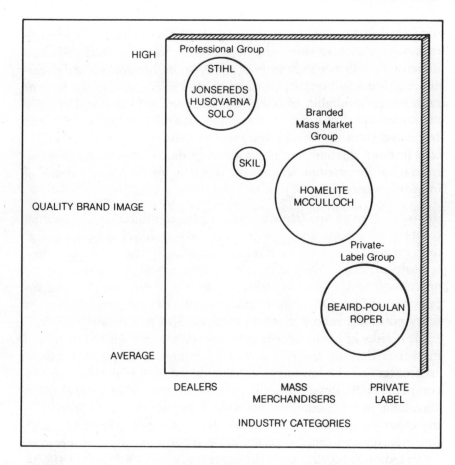

HIGH

Professional Group

STIHL

JONSEREDS
HUSQVARNA
SOLO

Branded
Mass Market
Group

SKIL

QUALITY BRAND IMAGE

HOMELITE
MCCULLOCH

Private-
Label Group

BEAIRD-POULAN
ROPER

AVERAGE

DEALERS   MASS
MERCHANDISERS   PRIVATE
LABEL

INDUSTRY CATEGORIES

Figure 4.7 Map of Strategic Groups in the U.S. Chain Saw Industry

There are many possible market definitions from which to choose a basis for market share measurement.   These alternatives are neither true nor false—only more or less useful for the purpose at hand.

Performance Evaluation and Short-Run Marketing Planning.   Here, the focus is on the presently served market, for this is the arena within which the organization is trying to satisfy customer needs. The priority is to find subgroups of customers with distinctive patterns of needs and responsiveness to marketing variables, in order to use these as a basis to gain and maintain a competitive advantage within the served market.   Such customer characteristics as industry type, volume requirements, reliance on technical service, and so forth provide useful bases for this kind of analysis.

Strategic Planning.   Broader market definitions are required to guide long-run resource allocation decisions and the assessment of relative cost positions.   Here, greater weight is given to "top-down" analyses of relative scale economies and shared experience in key cost sectors along the technology, function, and customer dimensions. Other indicators of appropriate boundaries are differences in industry maturity or stage of life cycle, stability of customer requirements, number of competitive entries and exits, and the rate of technological change. For example, useful strategic insights can be gained from the knowledge that the market for cheap car radios sold through discount outlets is growing much faster in some countries than the market served by specialty retail stores providing installation services.

Analysis of Threats and Opportunities. The identification of potential competitive threats and new venture opportunities requires a further broadening of the market definition. It is desirable to consciously uncouple the definition of the served market from the process of competitive surveillance or the search for new market opportunities. Otherwise, the bounds of current activity as reflected in the served market definition will perpetuate myopia.

The risks of such myopia are especially great when the served market is defined narrowly so as to minimize direct competitive confrontation. The unserved portion of the market is often used by competitors to develop scale and experience and to provide a launching pad for entry to the served market. This happened in the electrical transmission industry in the sixties.[12] Prior to 1960, this industry had little international competition, as producers concentrated on supplying their domestic markets. In the early 1960s, however, European manufacturers began to aggressively pursue U.S. contracts with power transformers that were lighter, used less oil, and yet were more efficient. They also offered advanced design "air-blast" circuit breakers much earlier than the U.S. suppliers. While the U.S. producers eventually matched these features, they had lost substantial market share by 1970. In retrospect, a major contributing factor to this loss was a narrow definition of their market, which excluded potential competitors. Many more recent examples illustrate such narrowness of vision, especially in regard to the potential threat of the Japanese in markets ranging from motorcycles to watches, ball bearings, and earth-moving equipment.

Multiple Units of Measurement. The performance of a product or a business may vary considerably depending on whether sales are

---

12. Epstein (1978).

measured in terms of dollars, units, or end users. The problem is particularly acute when large price differentials exist within the market. For example,[13] one company selling anti-asthma drugs had an

18% share of doctors prescribing
20% share of turnover (dollars)
30% share of all prescriptions written for anti-asthma drugs
40% share of all patients being treated

None of these share measures are sufficient on their own to reveal the competitive position of this drug company—especially the emphasis on heavy prescribers with relatively low prices. Also, if a single measure is emphasized, a temptation arises to select a definition to highlight whatever results management wants to present.

The methods and timing used to record sales and the definition of a relevant "sale" can also affect the measurement of market share. A study of the U.S. electrical apparatus industry [14] found:

> To a degree, the reported market shares could be managed up or down. There could be a genuine shift of market shares, or managers could create the temporary illusion of gains and losses by shifting the timing of their reported orders. This could be useful when preparing statistics for internal corporate consumption. The moment when an order was finally "booked" was often a matter of judgment. During periods of great organizational pressure for an increase in market share, operating managers had great incentive to report vague (and cancellable) commitments on the part of their (utility) customers, as if they were firm orders. By the same token, orders could be secretly hidden away, to be reported on a rainy day. [In this particular industry, where order backlogs are common, the] relevant strategy variable is share of orders, not share of shipments. Because of time lags, a decline in share of orders would not appear as a decline in share of shipments for several years. If managers focused their attention upon share of shipments in their strategic deliberations, they would be reacting to stale information—competitive intelligence several years obsolete.

To avoid potential misuse as well as strategic misguidance, it is desirable that all relevant dimensions of share be identified and the performance of the product and the business be assessed on all these measures.

---

13. Majaro (1977).
14. Sultan (1974).

Summary

Markets are complex, multidimensional arenas of competition composed of a myriad of niches and categories. The strategist seeking to understand a particular market is dealing with a moving target, for change is continuous along each of the key market dimensions of function, technology, customer segmentation, and degree of integration. Barriers to competitive movement along these dimensions are constantly shifting, creating both threats and opportunities for protected market positions.

Both top-down and bottom-up analyses of strategic markets are necessary to avoid myopic market definitions, for each approach has inherent deficiencies that need to be balanced by the contrasting perspective. A top-down emphasis on markets specified in terms of company capabilities and resources can blind one to threats from competitors who are outside the presently served market, or can mean delayed response to shifts in customer requirements or usage patterns. Conversely, markets defined solely from the customer's perspective may ignore crucial economic factors that dictate relative cost position, and may distort perceptions of opportunities in which the competencies and experience base of the company can effectively be employed.

An integrated analysis of strategic markets begins with the acceptance of a need for multiple market definitions, each more or less suitable for particular strategic or tactical issues. Generally, broad definitions are necessary for the analysis of new ventures or for competitive surveillance purposes, while narrower definitions are used for performance evaluation.

Developing Strategy Options: The Role of Generic Strategies

Strategy options are essential to the transition from the reflective and analytical mode of thinking that prevails during the situation assessment phase to the action-oriented decision and implementation phases of the planning process. An effective transition requires management to conceive and consider a broad array of future possibilities for the business. This helps overcome the narrowing of vision and uncritical acceptance of the present strategic direction that comes from premature closure on one option.

How Are Strategy Options Generated? One approach looks for inspiration from *generic* strategies, or generalized game plans, that seem to work in one industry after another. Some generic strategies are specific and deal with functional management actions for performance improvement, turnaround, harvesting, or divestment. Other generic strategy types describe broad patterns or combinations of functional actions, resource allocation, and competitive positions that characterize the way businesses tend to compete. In this chapter we will first describe a variety of generic management strategies and then consider broad generic competitive strategies. Some of these broad types of strategy have been found to be the basis for defensible competitive positions, while others are derived from a portfolio perspective.

Although generic strategies are useful for suggesting options and helping managers avoid pitfalls, they do not identify specific routes to competitive advantage that are grounded in the details of the market and competitive situation. Chapter 6 describes the kind of *strategic thinking* that is needed to match the capabilities of the business with the opportunities in the environment.

> *Today's chief executives don't have the menu to determine what their options are. They have to go out and search for the menu.*
>
> —*Herbert Simon*

Through this chapter and the next, we view the generation of strategic options as a creative activity that should not be prematurely channeled by critical evaluation. In practice, strategy development is iterative, for careful evaluation of the merits and limitations of the possible options can be used to suggest modifications and combinations of strategic options that minimize risk and maximize reward.

Generic Management Strategies

There are four basic types of management strategies:

1. Performance improvement strategies, emphasizing the possibilities for increasing sales volume;
2. Performance improvement strategies, oriented toward increasing profitability through improved productivity or margins;
3. Harvesting or divestment strategies; and
4. Turnaround strategies.

Each basic type has different implications for resource requirements, performance outcomes, and risk. Within these four types, many alternative strategic actions can be considered. There is a particularly rich array of possibilities for performance improvement, summarized in Figure 5.1. Each one is phrased in terms of fundamental action steps, so they are relatively easy to communicate across the organization and yet can be translated into functional decisions such as pricing, product quality, service levels, manufacturing processes, and human resource requirements. As will soon become evident, these generic management strategies are not mutually exclusive—many can and should be pursued in conjunction with others.[1]

Strategies to Increase Sales Volume

The generic options to increase sales volume are derived from the possibilities for expanding the business definition along one or more of the dimensions of the business definition. To illustrate

---

1. The classification in Figure 5.1 also ignores second-order effects, such as the consequences of increased sales volume for improved capacity utilization that will improve margins.

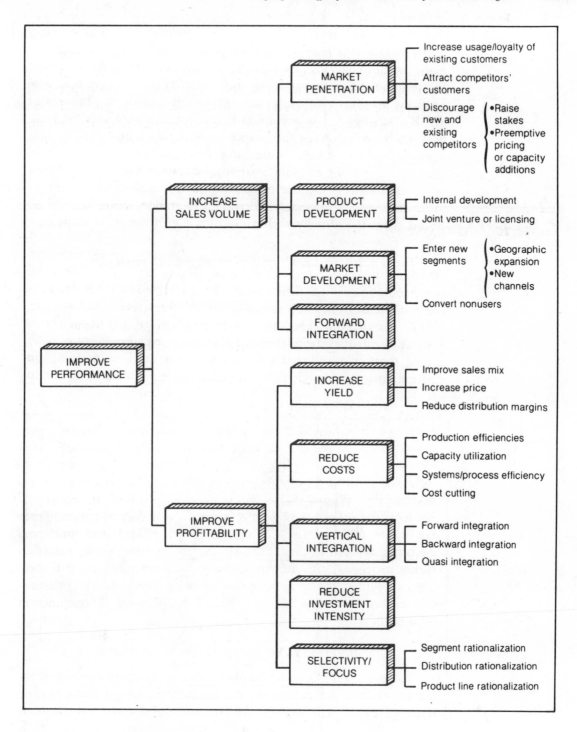

Figure 5.1 Generic Performance Improvement Strategies

these possibilities in Figure 5.2, we have treated the customer function dimension as representing the possibilities for product innovation, without giving explicit attention to the need for new technologies. Strictly speaking, the option of diversifying into new products serving completely new markets is outside the bounds of an SBU strategy. The exception is the situation in which the business has been set up for the purpose of entering a new market with a technology that is new to the company—essentially a new venture division. Another corporate strategy question that we have not considered here is the use of acquisitions to implement a management strategy. Conversely, forward integration along the value-added chain is normally within the purview of the SBU strategy.

Market Penetration. The market penetration class of management strategies involves much more than simply attracting customers from competitors. A direct attack on a competitor's customers is often the least desirable approach, for it invites retaliation that can nullify the initial gains and cause erosion of profit margins. Instead, the first priority should be to retain existing customers by giving them reasons to be loyal. In most markets, holding an existing customer rather than inducing a competitor's customer to

Figure 5.2 Directions for Expanding the Business Definition

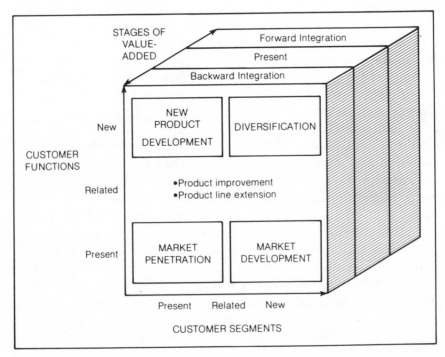

switch is demonstrably cheaper. This is most evident in consumer packaged goods markets in which a great deal of brand switching occurs. Consequently, most of the advertising budget is directed toward reinforcing awareness and attitudes of existing customers to ensure they do not defect. Another way to enhance loyalty and reduce price erosion is to be truly responsive to the customer's need for rapid or reliable delivery. This strategy, as executed by wholesalers who serve hardware and auto part dealers, requires both a willingness to maintain large stocks and a systematic delivery approach.

In high-growth markets, a market penetration objective may be best served by actively discouraging potential competitors from entering the market or existing competitors from attempting to gain share. The best-known form of this strategy is preemptive pricing, in which prices are set low in anticipation of future cost declines and even then will yield profits only for those few competitors with a significant experience base. This type of pricing is a prevalent and somewhat uncontrollable feature of the semiconductor and related industries. Preemption may also be achieved by building substantial capacity in excess of demand. Both prospective and potential competitors in highly capital-intensive industries may be deterred from investing in capacity additions if present utilization rates are low. When growth materializes, the business then has the capacity to serve the new requirements and thus to gain share when competition hits their capacity limit. Essentially, this strategy gave the Japanese suppliers a dominant position in the 64K random-access memory market in 1981. Their gain was at the expense of U.S. suppliers who had been reluctant to build too much excess capacity and could not respond quickly to a surge in demand.

Should a direct attack on competitors' customers be mounted, success is more assured if a combination of competitive factors is employed and primary emphasis is given to a few segments within the served market. One recent study [2] found that most businesses that achieved significant gains in share employed two or three factors in combination. For example, quality improvements and product changes were almost always reinforced with increases in promotion. The value of a balanced marketing program is well illustrated in the introduction of L'eggs pantyhose in 1971. The marketing strategy included several novel elements: a one-size product to fit most users, a new type of package, a special display

---

2. Buzzell and Wiersema (1981).

feature, and a new system of direct-to-the-store distribution that ensured L'eggs would seldom be out of stock. Heavy ~~advertising~~ and promotion were used to speed up consumer trial, and that in turn facilitated acceptance by retailers. As a result, L'eggs became the leading brand in the pantyhose market in 1974.

Most businesses that successfully gain share apparently do so by focusing their efforts on a few selected segments that are often relatively small at first. This was certainly the pattern in:

- the Miller Beer entry into the light beer segment,
- the Honda focus on a new type of motorcycle customer—the suburban, middle-class male—with a high-quality, small motorcycle,
- the entry by Savin and Canon into the office copier market with relatively low-priced, small machines suitable both for small users and for decentralized copying services in large organizations,
- the successful response by Airbus Industries to an unfilled gap in the market for wide-body commercial aircraft, with a medium range and medium capacity design, which was not offered by Boeing, McDonnell-Douglas, or Lockheed.

The probability of success of this strategy is enhanced when growth is significant in the entire industry or market and the established leaders are complacent, distracted by other challenges, or overly concerned about "cannibalization" of sales of the existing products by any new products they might offer.

Product Development. With a strategy of product development, the SBU remains within the present served market while either (1) extending the present product line, (2) improving the performance or perceived value of existing products, or (3) using a technology that is new to the firm to provide a new function to the served market. The first two options within this strategy are normally the least risky, as they build on the existing competencies of the organization. Other determinants of the risk of this strategy are the strategy role and timing of the new product introduction.

Various roles can be assigned to new products[3] including:

- utilize excess capacity
- combat a competitive entry

---

3. Kuczmarski and Silver (1982).

- exploit a new technology
- maintain a position as a product innovator
- protect market share

Within each of these roles, different entry strategies can be used. Some companies are consistently pioneeers with new technology, while others are conscious followers. Some who are fast followers achieve their competitive advantage by out-imitating. This requires an ability to respond fast and out-invest the pioneer. Another follower strategy is to leapfrog with a new technology. Northern Telecom did not simply emulate others in the market for electronic PBXs; instead, they jumped to a higher level of digital-switching technology that no one else had available. This strategy requires very strong R and D, and an ability to out-innovate the pioneer.

Product development strategies do not always fall neatly within the existing served market. Frequently, they also result in an entry into adjacent unserved market segments. This is especially evident in transitional industries such as computing, in which segment boundaries are fluid.

Market Development. There are two facets to the management strategy of market development. The first involves *entering new segments,* either by expanding the geographic base of the business (including international expansion) or by using new channels to reach unserved customers within the present geographic market. The benefits and risks will depend on the similarity of the new and present markets. If the degree of similarity of markets is high, then the additional volume will reduce unit costs by permitting better capacity utilization or larger scale operations. As the degree of similarity diminishes, the need both for product adaptation to serve new needs and for substantial marketing investments to reach the new market increases the risk considerably.

The second connotation of this strategy is the *conversion of nonusers of the product cate*gory. This possibility is especially significant during the early stages of the life cycle when much of the potential market has not tried or adopted the new product. The resource requirements can be substantial: nonuser segments are expensive to convert, prices may have to be lowered to attract price-sensitive segments, and considerable fixed and working capital is required to keep pace with the resultant growth. These considerations will be explored in much greater depth in the chapter of the companion volume dealing with product life cycle analysis.

Forward Integration.   The potential gains from a forward integration strategy depend at the outset on how close the business is to the ultimate consumer.   If the value-added chain is long, the business has the option of integrating one or more of the activities, such as assembly, service, inventorying, merchandising, financing, or distributing, depending on where it is currently located.   The motivations are to achieve more effective distribution coverage, reduce uncertainty, or increase control.   Among the possible outcomes are reduced marketing and servicing costs, lower production costs because production schedules are more stable, and increased sales. These outcomes will be worthwhile only if competition with present customers is not severe or extra costs are not incurred because of the necessity of a full line.   Forward integration is sometimes the only way to reach the market if existing channels are already locked up by competitors.

Strategies to Improve Profitability

If profitability is defined broadly as return on assets managed or net investment, then the relevant opportunities for improvement can be identified by decomposing the profitability measure.   (Figure 5.3).   Thus, the avenues to profit improvement are: increase sales volume or sales *yield* (the realized price per unit), reduce *costs*

Figure 5.3 Components of Profitability

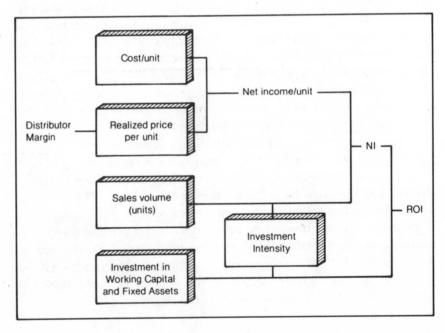

per unit, or reduce the *investment intensity* (the number of dollars of sales per dollar of investment in fixed and working capital).

Increasing the Sales Yield.   The purpose of increasing the sales yield is to achieve the highest average price per unit across the product line. The essential ingredient is detailed knowledge of unit profitability after reasonable allocations of costs to each product and market segment. With this knowledge, action can be taken to shift the sales mix toward high-profit items by such steps as differential commission rates. At the same time, gross margins can be adjusted through price changes to reflect the extent of competition encountered by each product. High-gross margins should be sought from products facing limited direct competition, while margins on highly competitive commodity products should be low (Figure 5.4). The option of an across-the-board price increase, versus the selective item increases proposed above, is riskier as it exposes the business to market share losses if the competitors do not follow. Also risky is an attempt to increase price at the expense of distributor margins, unless it is accompanied by a reduction of some of the distributor's functions or provision of other benefits.

Unit-Cost Reduction.   A wide gamut of strategies is available to reduce unit cost, including:

- improving production efficiencies. This can be done through standardization of design, components, and processes, coupled with mechanization of labor-intensive activities.

- cutting material costs by substituting new materials and finding or developing lower cost sources or perhaps subcontracting out elements of the production process.

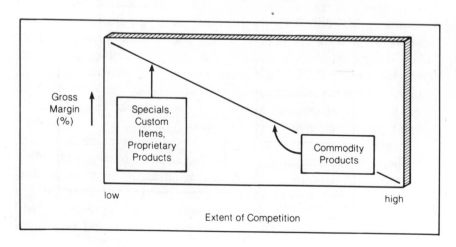

Figure 5.4 Adjusting Gross Margins to Extent of Competition

- enhancing buying power. To extract concessions from suppliers, many firms pool the purchases of a number of business units. Similarly, retail grocery chains form buying groups to qualify for volume discounts.

- improving systems and process efficiency by adopting new process technology or by using computer-aided planning and control systems, as well as providing for improved work flow patterns and improving management information systems.

- increasing capacity utilization. This option is especially compelling in high fixed-cost industries. When capacity utilization dips below the break-even point, the business should be prepared to seek new volume to fill the plant by reducing price, extending payment terms, adding services, or withdrawing capacity rather than taking on unprofitable sales.

The epitome of a wide-ranging cost reduction strategy is demonstrated by Iowa Beef Processors. Within two decades, the company was transformed from a small, regional meat packer to the dominant competitor in the industry. Their strategy was to move butchering from the retail store to their factories and to pay meticulous attention to each cost element, including slaughtering, transportation, and marketing, in order to sustain a competitive cost advantage. They also trimmed waste by finding new markets for cattle hides, fat, bone, and even gallstones.

Vertical Integration. The virtues of backward integration are similar to those of forward integration—better control and lower costs. Control in this context means assurance of supply during periods of scarcity as well as protection against concomitant price increases. Thus, during the seventies, Dow Chemical prepared for the energy crisis by putting almost half of its energy requirements under its control, either by direct ownership of supplies or through such arrangements as owning pipelines that connect independently owned natural gas fields with its plants.

A major motivation for vertical integration is to reduce costs. This happens if many of the transaction costs of buying and selling incurred when separate companies own adjacent stages of production can be eliminated when the companies or functions are merged. Further cost reduction may come from improved coordination of production output, inventory scheduling, and marketing programs.[4] Thus an in-house supplier has an opportunity to schedule production more efficiently when it has firm commitments from a "downstream" manufacturing or distribution facility.

Vertical integration has costs and risks that may offset the anticipated benefits. This strategy requires scarce capital that might have a higher yield elsewhere. It is also risky to the extent it increases exposure to fluctuations in a specific market. This is fine if the market is healthy because profits will be enhanced; but should it turn down, integration will cause profits to be more depressed than otherwise. A further risk is that integration will raise exit barriers. The additional investment and related commitments make it more difficult to contemplate exiting the business.

To the extent that integration implies commitment to a particular technology or manufacturing system, it reduces flexibility of response to market or technology changes. In the 1960s, Jonathan Logan, a women's apparel manufacturer, was so committed to double-knit fabrics that it invested in a textile mill. Although double knits abruptly went out of fashion, Jonathan Logan continued to use them to absorb the capacity of the captive mill. The mill was finally closed in 1981, and the company reported a $40 million write-off.[5]

The attractiveness of a vertical integration strategy depends on the nature of the value-added chain and the competitive advantages of the different participants in the chain. For example, in the following value-added system, an efficient manufacturer of compo-

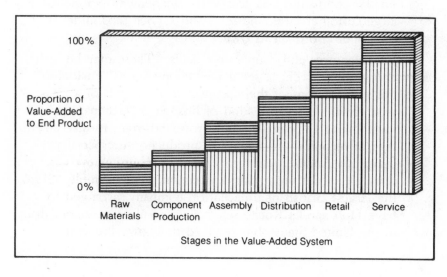

Figure 5.5 Stages in the Value-Added System

4. Buzzell (1983).

5. Adapted from Buzzell (1983).

nents might be tempted to integrate forward if the assembler seems inefficient.[6] The small valueadded during the component production stage, however, reduces the likelihood that an assembler will be interested in backward integration.

Quasi-Integration.   These represent efforts to gain some of the benefits of vertical integration without the constraints and capital commitments of 100 percent ownership of the adjacent member of the value-added chain.   Three types of quasi-integrated linkages are possible:

- Long term contracts link buyers and sellers for a number of transactions, and for long periods of time. This is the loosest type of quasi-integration because the negotiations on contract terms are set by inter-firm negotiations that are similar in character to arm's-length transactions.

- Financial alignments may consist of minority equity ownership, long-term debt financing between a buyer (such as a steel mill) and a seller (such as a coal mine), or prepurchase credits. These alignments have become very popular in high technology markets. Large companies such as IBM have been making minority investments in telecommunications (ROLM) and semiconductors (Intel). This gives them access to the talents of the smaller companies who otherwise would not choose to be acquired. The smaller company gains access to management experience, a large customer base, and sales and service capabilities it could not afford on its own.[7]

- Joint ventures and cooperative deals. These may be technologically driven; a seller may cooperate to "custom-fit" the specifications of their product to the needs of a user, or vice versa. Often this kind of linkage is accompanied by joint R and D programs and process changes to take advantage of technical efficiencies in production or specialized logistics. Another variant of this linkage is achieved through a joint promotion agreement. For example, Glaxo, the largest British pharmaceutical company, arranged to have Hoffman-La Roche sell their new ulcer treatment drug in the United States, but retained their own brand name

---

6. Grant and King (1982).

7. "Suddenly U.S. Companies Are Teaming Up" *Business Week* (11 July 1983) 71–74.

for the drug rather than licensing the compound as is usually the case.[8]   The benefit to Glaxo was access to an aggressive sales force of 700 to promote the product to tens of thousands of physicians and hospitals.   The existing Glaxo U.S. sales force of 450 was simply not large enough for the task.   Roche wanted the agreement because its patent on Valium was to run out in 1985, and an extra source of revenue was needed to ease the transition to a new family of products.

In general, businesses in a strong bargaining position can use quasi-integration to control the activities of external suppliers or customers as if they were owned.   Thus, this strategy can be a relatively inexpensive way to leverage the breadth of operations.   Joint ventures can provide R and D or marketing capabilities the business could not afford on its own.   Franchising contracts can enable the business to control the quality of its product or service.   Long-term take-or-pay contracts can provide a buffer to market uncertainty.

Reduce Investment Intensity.   A pervasive characteristic of investment-intensive businesses is low average profitability.[9]   The reason is partly arithmetical: investment intensity means that the denominator in the ROI ratio will be large.   A more significant factor is the pressure for high levels of capacity utilization in industries in which significant assets are required to support a dollar of sales. This volume orientation triggers serious price erosion when average capacity utilization declines in industries such as pulp and paper, commodity chemicals, and nonferrous metals.   Investment intensity, however, is also a problem in industries in which high levels of working capital are required.   Significant profit improvement can consequently be achieved by:

- reducing inventories, including work-in-process.
- reducing accounts receivable.
- recognizing the strategic consequences of capital-intensifying investments in systems and automation.   Specifically, will these investments yield a competitive advantage by increasing material yields or achieving service and quality levels not available to the competition, or will they primarily reduce flexibility?

---

8. Dreyfuss (1983).
9. Schoeffler (1978).

- subcontracting elements of the production process that require significant capital commitments.
- developing captive volume that can ensure the capital-intensive facility is loaded at or near the optimal capacity utilization level.

Seldom can this avenue for profit improvement be pursued without consideration of other revenue enhancement strategies. For example, efforts to reduce investment intensity may have an adverse effect on quality of service if low inventories mean immediate delivery is no longer possible, or they may be perceived as a hidden price increase if credit terms are more stringent.

Selectivity/Focus Strategies. Profitability can often be enhanced by consciously reducing the scope of the operation to the most profitable elements and accepting a decline in revenue and volume. This is sometimes called the "little jewel" strategy. Rationalization and retrenchment can occur along any or all the dimensions of the business definition:

- Market segment rationalization involves pruning back to concentrate the marketing focus. For small-share firms, the most attractive segments are those in which a small scale of operations hurts the least, such as protected regional markets, segments that attach a high importance to service or quality, or where the investment intensity is low.
- Product line rationalization, in which the line is significantly narrowed, is usefully pursued in conjunction with concentration on particular segments.
- Distribution rationalization is a pruning of the distribution system to a more effective network; this may include dropping small-volume outlets or limiting sales coverage to chains with central buying committees.

Strategies for Special Circumstances

The generic management strategies we have discussed so far are most appropriate to businesses in which the investment thrust is either to build, focus, or maintain the position. They must be adapted considerably when the business is being *harvested* to maximize short-run cash flow, *divested* or liquidated, or *turned around* to avoid potential failure.

Harvesting Strategies.   Unfortunately, harvesting strategies have acquired the unhappy connotation of ultimate surrender in the minds of many managers.   To a degree, this is an accurate perception for businesses or products in a weak position, in which the harvesting is *aggressive.*   A *thin* harvesting option is also available, which is appropriate for leaders in mature or declining markets who are reaping the rewards of past investment.   The purpose is to redeploy the business's cash flow to other areas of the business that have greater appetites for capital and more attractive growth prospects. In this latter option, the business or product-market unit is being managed for positive cash flow without a significant loss of market position.   The focus here is on the generic management strategies for profit improvement that avoid large capital expenditures.

The features of an aggressive harvesting strategy are fairly clearcut.   Operating costs are reduced to a bare-bones level through stringent cost cutting.   Capital expenditures are limited to essential replacements or government mandated safety and pollution control equipment.   Specific steps include raising prices, cutting sales and promotion expenditures, reducing customer service levels, and cutting back and de-emphasizing research and engineering.[10]

Although an aggressive harvest calls for reduced budgets and cost cutting, it is important to avoid signaling the intention of the strategy to either customers or competitors.   Otherwise, the decline in sales will be even sharper and the desired cash flow benefits may not be gained.   This means the first cutbacks should be in the less visible areas of R and D and facilities.   Only later should service levels and advertising be noticeably reduced.

Turnaround Strategies.   Turnaround strategies are employed to arrest and reverse a serious decline in the profitability and market position of the business.   The presumption is that the business has sufficient long-run potential to be worth saving, but the short-term problems could be fatal unless immediately corrected.   The first priority is to get cash flow under control by stretching payables, cutting inventories, increasing labor productivity, selling surplus capacity, cutting discretionary expenses, and so forth.   At the same time, tight financial controls must be put in place to ensure that information on the financial situation is timely and meaningful. Once some breathing time is available, an accurate determination of the reasons for the decline is critical.   Is it the result of an ineffec-

---

10. Rothschild (1979).

tive strategy, or is it poor execution? Are the causes of decline beyond management control? One study [11] found that 74 percent of turnaround situations were due to poor execution. When the strategy is wrong, then all the performance improvement options in Figure 5.1 need to be explored. If the problems are with operations, then a strategy change may also be desirable, but a more likely response is to improve the efficiency and effectiveness of implementation. The most typical operating responses beyond emergency cost cutting were found to be major plant construction or expansion, price and promotion changes, and asset deployment. These responses were almost always accompanied by major management changes.

Generic Competitive Strategies

These generic strategies describe the overall patterns of management actions and resource commitments needed to achieve one of the following defensible competitive positions:

- overall cost leadership
- differentiation from competition
- focus on a protected niche

The characteristics of these competitive positions and the supporting skills and resources were described in Chapter 2. Certainly the basic notion is appealing because it is robust and yields intuitive insights into successful strategic actions. Like all generalized frameworks, however, the real value comes from knowing how to adapt the notion to the circumstances at hand. This is the primary concern of this section.

Determinants of
Generic Competitive Strategies

According to Strategic Planning Associates, two factors within an industry will significantly constrain the choice of generic strategy. The first factor is *customer price sensitivity,* ranging from high—because the product is expensive or is a large element of their budget—to low—meaning the product is inexpensive or a small item in

---

11. Schendel, Patton, and Riggs (1976).

the budget.   The second factor is the customer's *perceived differentiation* among products in the market—the extent to which a significant difference is present between competitors' products—a difference they are willing to pay for.

The positioning of products on these two factors may depend on segment differences.   For example, business buyers of personal computers place greater demands on both hardware and software than do most home buyers.   As a result, they are likely to perceive greater differences among competitive offerings.   Home buyers, however, are likely to be more price sensitive, because the total system accounts for a large part of their discretionary budget.

The feasible combinations of price sensitivity and perceived differentiation, shown in Figure 5.6, suggest situations in which the generic cost leadership, differentiation, or focus strategies are likely to be most appropriate.   This portrayal of generic strategies highlights the need to continually adapt the strategy to evolving circumstances.   For example, a niche or focus strategy depends on the buyer's perception of meaningful differences among competitive products, which can change as imitation narrows differences and buyers become more sophisticated.   This is essentially the problem confronting the Hyster Company—long a profitable maker of top-of-the-line forklift trucks, with the most powerful engines, fastest lift speeds, and tightest turning radii.   This niche has narrowed as Japanese producers have entered with reliable, cheaper forklifts with heavy lifting capabilities.   Hyster's response has been to shift to the

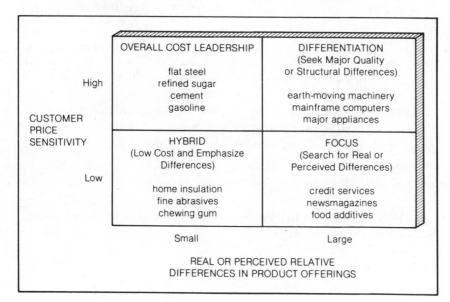

Figure 5.6 Determinants of Generic Strategies

low end of the market with a low-cost and low-price thrust. One element of this strategy is a large, new, automated plant in Northern Ireland with low labor costs and significant potential for economies of scale.[12]

Composite Strategies

The hybrid strategy shown in Figure 5.6 suggests that situations exist in which it is desirable to pursue both differentiated and low-cost positions at the same time. This approach is somewhat at odds with the conventional wisdom that sees these two generic positions as basically incompatible.[13] The rationale for this presumed incompatibility is that higher quality usually requires the use of more expensive components and less standardized production processes that increase costs. Also, higher communications expenditures may be necessary to convey a quality position, and sales force expenses may be higher to support technical services.

Recent evidence suggests that the dichotomy between high quality and low cost is misleading in many situations. One study has raised the possibility that product quality has an indirect lowering influence on direct costs via its effects on market position.[14] The evidence is that higher quality results in higher market share, which in turn lowers direct costs due to scale economies and experience effects. Quality may also have a direct positive effect on total costs. Those who advocate the notion that "quality is free" have persuasive evidence that the costs of higher quality standards are offset by lower reject rates, lower costs of make-good and field repairs, and greater customer satisfaction.

In reality, the presumed choice between reducing cost versus building in more value to customers is seldom so clear-cut as the generic competitive strategies would suggest. Instead, most strategies are a balanced mix of the generic alternatives.

Different definitions of the market are a useful first step toward illuminating the appropriate strategic balance. What is sought is a perspective on relative competitive position that reflects both supply and demand factors:

---

12. Hyster: A Top-of-the-Line Producer Tries to Beat Japan at its Own Game," *Business Week* (8 February 1982).

13. Hall (1980) and Porter (1980).

14. Phillips, Chang, and Buzzell (1983).

1. A *supply* perspective requires broadly drawn market boundaries—often corresponding to conventional industry boundaries based on similarity of production process or raw material, as discussed in Chapter 4. The market definition should encompass related products and activities that influence the experience base, and the ability to achieve economies of scale. Share of this market is an indicator of unit production and distribution costs, relative to competitors.

2. A *demand* perspective uses narrower, customer-oriented definitions to gain insights into how a differentiated competitive position is converted into either premium prices or lower marketing costs. These advantages are normally achieved within specific end-use or consumption segments, and their attainment is best measured by the relative share of these segments. Very high shares of a few segments is evidence of effective focus or positioning to meet the needs of distinct target groups. These segments are very profitable, for they are frequently willing to pay a premium price for a perceived quality advantage that exceeds the incremental cost of providing the added value, and may be less expensive to reach with marketing programs because they are more loyal buyers.

The central air conditioner market illustrates how supply and demand factors work together to determine relative profitability. Manufacturers with high perceived quality and ability to provide continuing service support are in a particularly good margin position in the home modernization segment, which values these attributes and is willing to pay a premium for them. These manufacturers, however, cannot avoid also serving the less profitable, highly price-sensitive new construction market. Average unit manufacturing cost is determined by the combined volume of sales in the two end-use segments.

The two broad avenues to profitability are combined in Figure 5.7. The importance of supply factors relative to demand factors can differ dramatically, depending on perceived differences among products and the ability of competitors to match any cost advantages or .o provide equivalent customer values. This in turn will determine the degree of emphasis to place on the pursuit of overall cost leadership versus the achievement of a differentiated position in the served market.

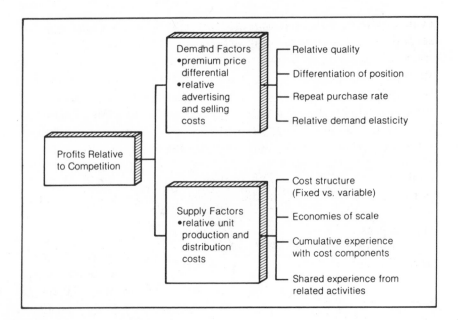

Figure 5.7 Sources of Profitability

Portfolio Perspectives on Generic Strategies

The essence of portfolio models is the classification of business or product markets within a two-dimensional matrix, in which one dimension represents the *attractiveness of the market,* and the other dimension is the *strength of the competitive position.* The Appendix to this chapter describes the construction of portfolio matrices. As the same dimensions of evaluation are applied to all businesses, it is possible to directly compare the portfolio position of all the SBUs within the company. It is also possible to consider each SBU as managing its own portfolio—not of different businesses but of product markets that may have diverse positions within the matrix. The position of an SBU in the matrix has direct implications for the generic investment strategy of the business—that is, whether it is in a "invest/build," "hold," or "harvest" mode.

Most companies adopt a portfolio perspective to cope with the diversity of their operations and to avoid the extremes of stifling centralization of strategy formulation versus dangerous decentralization. Initial interest is facilitated by the intuitively appealing notion that long-run corporate performance is more than the sum of the contributions of the individual businesses, plus the insights and communicability of simple matrix displays.

Three distinct patterns of usage have emerged. One group of companies uses portfolio matrices simply as *diagnostic aids* that can be used to synthesize prior strategic judgments, focus issues, and evaluate the current or prospective position of the business unit. A second group of companies uses portfolio models as the basis for a *system of management,* encompassing the assignment of investment strategies to businesses, the allocation of resources, and the evaluation of performance. There is a third, intermediate pattern of usage, in which the portfolio model serves as a *framework* to facilitate the generation of strategic options that recognize the financial interrelationships among businesses and products, but does not prescribe the choice of option. A 1979 survey of Fortune 1000 companies [15] estimated that 36 percent of the companies had adopted a portfolio approach and that the number of users was growing at 15 to 20 percent per year. Close to half the adopters were using the approach as the basis for a management system.

A representative market attractiveness and business strength portfolio matrix is shown in Figure 5.8.[16] The details of how to

Figure 5.8 Strategic Options

	strong	**medium**	**weak**
high	**PROTECT POSITION** •invest to grow at maximum digestible rate •concentrate effort on maintaining strength	**INVEST TO BUILD** •challenge for leadership •build selectively on strengths •reinforce vulnerable areas	**BUILD SELECTIVELY** •specialize around limited strengths •seek ways to overcome weaknesses •withdraw if indications of sustainable growth are lacking
medium	**BUILD SELECTIVELY** •invest heavily in most attractive segments •build up ability to counter competition •emphasize profitability by raising productivity	**SELECTIVITY/MANAGE FOR EARNINGS** •protect existing program •concentrate investments in segments where profitability is good and risk is relatively low	**LIMITED EXPANSION OR HARVEST** •look for ways to expand without high risk; otherwise, minimize investment and rationalize operations
low	**PROTECT AND REFOCUS** •manage for current earnings •concentrate on attractive segments •defend strengths	**MANAGE FOR EARNINGS** •protect position in most profitable segments •upgrade product line •minimize investment	**DIVEST** •sell at time that will maximize cash value •cut fixed costs and avoid investment meanwhile

MARKET ATTRACTIVENESS (vertical axis) — COMPETITIVE POSITION (horizontal axis)

15. Haspeslagh (1982).

16. This is a composite of matrices from several sources including Abell and Hammond (1979), Ohmae (1982), and Robinson, Hickens, and Wade (1978).

construct this type of matrix can be found in the appendix to this chapter. Distinct generic strategy implications are associated with each of the nine cells in the matrix. These correspond to the investment strategy alternatives that describe one leg of an overall strategic thrust (as discussed in Chapter 2). The emphasis on this facet of the thrust of the strategy is consistent with primary use of portfolio matrices for guiding resource allocations within the firm. Each of the investment strategies, however, also implies several generic management strategies.

One of the dangers of these portfolio classification matrices is that an individual business or product becomes an impersonal dot in a matrix, characterized only by static, quantifiable measures along two dimensions. The resources and objectives to be assigned to business A versus business B then become a matter of the relative attractiveness of their positions in the matrix. This mechanistic perspective can be overcome if care is taken to understand the reasons for the position of the business in the matrix, and then to search for creative ways to improve the position of the business. For this purpose, it is desirable to show the anticipated consequences of the alternative investment thrusts in the portfolio. These alternatives also shift the relative emphasis from one dimension of the portfolio matrix to the other, as shown in the following examples:

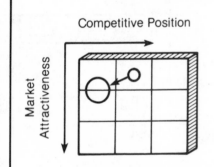

Invest to build: This strategy option is indicated when a highly attractive market offers opportunities for growth that may not be available as the market matures. Significant investments are required to build selectively on strengths and keep up with the rapid growth rates that are typical of these markets.

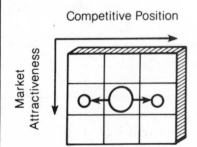

Selectivity/manage for earnings: Here, the indicated option is to strengthen the position of the business in segments where profitability is good or barriers to competitive entry can be maintained, while letting the position erode in segments where costs exceed benefits.

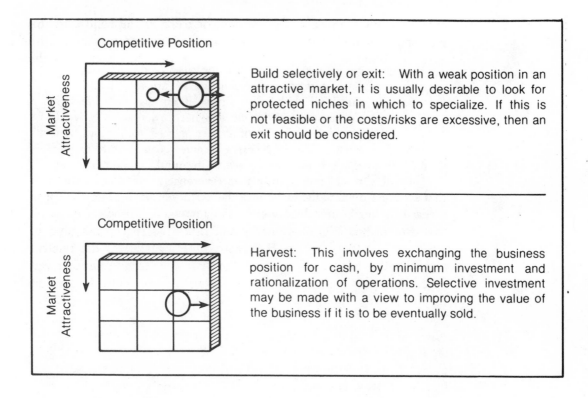

Build selectively or exit: With a weak position in an attractive market, it is usually desirable to look for protected niches in which to specialize. If this is not feasible or the costs/risks are excessive, then an exit should be considered.

Harvest: This involves exchanging the business position for cash, by minimum investment and rationalization of operations. Selective investment may be made with a view to improving the value of the business if it is to be eventually sold.

The Role of Generic Strategies

The array of generic strategies serves primarily as a framework within which one can think about the strategic possibilities for the business unit. This thinking is facilitated by having a common language that all members of the management team can use to describe both the current strategy and the options that should be considered. The relevant options will depend on the specific situation as defined by the portfolio position. As we saw in the review of portfolio options, the feasibility of the various generic options is generally dictated by such factors as the stage in the life cycle, the market position of the business, and the resources available.

Consideration of generic options still leaves us far short of the specification of specific action steps and resource deployments that will secure a competitive advantage in an individual situation. Thus, it is only the beginning step in the process of generating strategic options. To fully articulate these options, we must dig more deeply into the details of the situation. This stage in the analysis is highly creative and can be facilitated by the methods and concepts described in the next chapter.

In summary, there is a great deal of truth in the following story [17] which is ignored by strategists at their own peril:

> Strategic concepts may be a bit like the rules of the Assassins. That curious medieval sect of Muslim fanatics, we are told, had several orders or ranks, each with its own place in an ascending hierarchy. Upon being promoted into the next highest order, initiates would be given a new, and presumably loftier, set of rules to live by. After years during which these structures became second nature to them, the devout might even find a place in the ninth, or highest order. These few would wait with hushed reverence as the sect's leader welcomed them individually into the elect, whispering into the ear of each the final, ultimate wisdom. The message: "There are no rules."

---

17. Kiechel (1979).

Constructing the Portfolio Classification Matrix

The sources of information that are the basis for the market attractiveness and business strength matrix are summarized in Figure 5.9.

Underlying this model is the notion that market or industry attractiveness should reflect differences in the *average* level of long-run profit potential for all participants in the market, while differences along the competitive position dimension should be related to the profitability of the business *relative* to the competition. This is a static picture that will deteriorate over time unless new sources of advantage are found. Hence, it is desirable to classify a business or product market on both dimensions, both in the present and in the future.

The major difference among standardized portfolio models is whether they use a single factor—such as the market share/growth matrix—or multiple factors to represent the two dimensions. Each has its own merits and limitations that will be dealt with fully in a companion volume in this series. Substantial consensus exists, however, that for diagnostic purposes, the multiple factor approach is superior. The following sequence of steps is used to develop all multifactor portfolio models:

1. Establish level and units of analyses (business units or product markets or both).

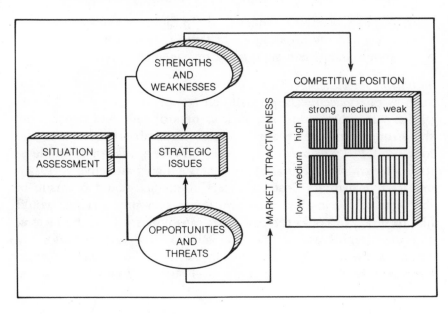

Figure 5.9 Portfolio Classification Matrix

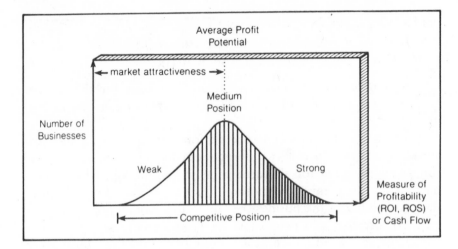

Figure 5.10
Determinants of
Profitability

2. Identify factors underlying the market attractiveness and competitive position dimensions.

3. Assign weights to factors to reflect their relative importance.

4. Assess the *current* position of each SBU or PMU on each factor.

5. Aggregate individual factor judgments into an overall score reflecting the current position of the SBU or PMU on the two classification dimensions.

6. Repeat the process for subsequent years in the planning period, assuming a continuation of the current strategy.

7. Explore possible changes in the position of each of the units and the implications of these changes for resource requirements and supporting management strategies.

Identifying the Factors.   In some industries or market environments, such as pharmaceuticals, virtually all competitors achieve adequate profits. In other industries, such as tires or pulp and paper, only the strongest competitors will report acceptable profits over the long run. For purposes of diagnosis, however, it is not desirable to use such extreme cases to define what is a highly attractive versus an unattractive market. Instead, these judgments should be made in the light of the markets the company is presently serving, would like to serve, or could serve with its capabilities. Thus the factors, and the weights assigned to the factors, will vary considerably among a financial services company such as Shearson/American Express, a semiconductor manufacturer such as Texas Instruments, and a company primarily in industrial and consumer products based on chemicals and plastic, such as DuPont. Although each of these companies is diversified, there is sufficient relationship among the SBUs that the factors underlying market attractiveness and competitive position are meaningful for each SBU. Conglomerates find the portfolio concept unattractive, for the lack of relationship among the businesses makes comparisons on standard factors difficult if not impossible.

Two complementary approaches to identifying factors can be used to evaluate all the businesses or product markets in the portfolio. One approach is to select from a standard checklist, such as Table 5.1, those factors that have historically been determinants of industry profitability or relative profitability.[18] Another approach is to select several pairs of businesses, in which one member of each pair is a priori agreed to be a very unattractive business, and the other is very attractive to the company. Factors can then be derived by identifying the important differences between the two businesses.

Relating the Factors to the Dimensions. Each factor may increase or decrease market attractiveness or competitive position. The relationship is frequently complex. For example, is a competitive structure with a few large competitors of the same size superior to a situation in which there are many smaller competitors? What constitutes a rapid growth rate? In the chemical industry, expansion of capacity is often constrained by uncertainty of feedstock supply. If this is the case, or if there are competing uses for the feedstocks, the market is regarded as attractive. Conversely, if there is a surplus of feedstock, suppliers of the feedstock may reduce prices or invest in more capacity to increase consumption. This situation is unattractive.[19] As these examples suggest, a great deal of judgment and analysis may be necessary before accurate judgments on the relationship of factors with dimensions can be made.

---

18. Many of these factors have been suggested by the PIMS study (Profit Impact of Market Strategies), which is reviewed in depth in a companion volume.

19. Robinson, Hichens, and Wade (1978).

Table 5.1 Factors Contributing to Market Attractiveness and Competitive Position (Adapted from Abell and Hammond 1979)

ATTRACTIVENESS OF YOUR BUSINESS	STRENGTH OF YOUR COMPETITIVE POSITION
A. Market Factors ■ size (dollars, units) ■ size of product market ■ market growth rate ■ stage in life cycle ■ diversity of market (potential for differentiation) ■ price elasticity ■ bargaining power of customers ■ cyclicality/seasonality of demand B. Economic and Technological Factors ■ investment intensity ■ nature of investment (facilities, working capital, leases) ■ ability to pass through effects of inflation ■ industry capacity ■ level and maturity of technology utilization ■ barriers to entry/exit ■ access to raw materials C. Competitive Factors ■ types of competitors ■ structure of competition ■ substitution threats ■ perceived differentiation among competitors D. Environmental Factors ■ regulatory climate ■ degree of social acceptance ■ human factors such as unionization	A. Market Position ■ relative share of market ■ rate of change of share ■ variability of share across segments ■ perceived differentiation of quality/price/service ■ breadth of product ■ company image B. Economic and Technological Position ■ relative cost position ■ capacity utilization ■ technological position ■ patented technology, product, or process C. Capabilities ■ management strength and depth ■ marketing strength ■ distribution system ■ labor relations ■ relationships with regulators

Creative Thinking about Strategy Options

A recurring theme to criticisms of strategic planning practice is the pedestrian quality of the strategic options that are considered. The mind-set of management is too often shaped and narrowed by the uncritical acceptance of dubious assumptions and by the unwillingness to step beyond the familiar bounds of the present strategy. When management is challenged to produce options, they respond with thinly disguised "straw men" that cannot be given serious consideration. The options that remain in contention are frequently variations on the same theme. The consequent predictability of action and lack of foresight can readily be exploited by astute competitors.

Fool you are . . . to say you learn by your experience . . . I prefer to profit by other's mistakes, and avoid the price of my own.

—Bismarck

Some argue that the planning process itself inhibits creativity. "In many companies, the process of proposing a new idea, justifying it and defending it against 'challenges' by corporate staff and senior management is so intimidating that all but the most confident entrepreneurs are inclined to stick to less imaginative approaches that are easier to quantify and defend." [1] Clearly, many factors contribute to this state of affairs, including nonsupportive review systems, internal competition for leadership or credit, excessively rigid organization structures, and managers with a short-run response orientation.

Many of these inhibiting factors are rooted in the organization, traditions, and culture of the firm, and fall outside the scope of this book. Their deadening effects, however, can be reduced through careful management of the planning process to encourage the development of creative options. Such a planning process succeeds in this end, primarily by providing a supportive climate. This can be achieved through the conscious separation of strategic option gener-

---

1. Hunsicker (1980).

ation from evaluation, coupled with full participation from all levels of management. The specifics of planning systems designed to achieve these ends are discussed in Chapter 8.

Strategic Thought-Triggers. The effectiveness of the planning process is further enhanced with conceptual approaches that systematically encourage strategic thinking about changes in the determinants of competitive success and how these changes can be exploited or deliberately shaped. A variety of such "thought-triggers" is available to be adapted to the specific needs and situation of a business. The purpose of this chapter is to describe and elaborate five approaches that have proved effective in a variety of situations:

- Challenge the present strategy
- Look for strategic windows
- Play on competitors' vulnerabilities
- Change the rules of the competitive game
- Enhance customer value

These approaches are highly complementary; there is no invariant order in which to apply them. Also, some are more appropriate than others in specific circumstances.

Challenge the Present Strategy

For a business in the midst of a major strategy review—following the steps outlined in the earlier chapters—an appropriate departure point for strategic thinking is the present strategy. Significant benefits often arise simply from articulating all the elements of this strategy, which frequently represents the net effect of having grasped a number of unexpected opportunities, taken some deals and rejected others, responded to urgent needs for correcting errors, and juggled resource commitments in response to changing needs and internal political pressures. The full implications of these sequences of short-run adaptations are often not recognized and may not be viewed as desirable when recognized. Once the present strategy has been articulated, a variety of approaches can be employed to challenge underlying assumptions and future viability.

Assess Competitiveness

Although a complete statement of the current strategy should specify the basis for competitive advantage, it is essential that the assumptions and data underlying this judgment be subjected to rigorous testing. This is especially important with businesses that have been successful in the past. Success tends to reinforce the belief of management in the essential correctness of past approaches and the present competitive posture. As Henderson notes, however, "So long as the underlying competitive conditions and relationships continue to hold, the corporate success may also continue. But in time these conditions must change." [2]

To avoid such myopia, corporate-level management must be prepared to challenge the business: "If, as you say, our competitors are three years away from introducing microprocessors in their control units, why are they already talking about it in their annual reports?" "What cost savings could customers achieve with microprocessor controlled equipment?" These challenges expose faulty data and unfounded assumptions, and clearly establish the importance of a sustainable competitive advantage.

In preparation for this kind of questioning, management of the business needs to examine their competitive position from several vantage points. Useful aids to thinking include the in-depth analysis of segment market shares described in Chapter 4, combined with research evidence on customer perceptions of advantages, as discussed in Chapter 2. Another approach is a role reversal in which managers put themselves in the position of their strongest competitor. In this role they can ask themselves, "If I were to attack our business, where would I find the least resistance? How would I attack? Do I have the resources to carry out such an attack?" The answers to such questions lead logically to thinking about action to buttress the business against attacks on vulnerable positions.

Find Areas of Leverage. One company probes the unexploited potential of the present strategy by posing the following questions during their planning process:

Suppose you could have another $1 million to put into your business in any way you see fit, but with the understanding that you would

---

2. Henderson (1979).

be held accountable, five years hence, for having used the money well. How would you spend or invest the money? On more sales-men? More efficient plant? Advertising? New product development?

The answers are revealing, especially when they expose cross-functional differences in perspective and an all too frequent lack of good understanding of the responsiveness of the market to strategic initiatives.

Minimize Contingencies

Contingencies are (1) low-probability events that (2) could have significant consequences in terms of damage or missed opportunities and (3) have to be dealt with quickly if the event occurs. For example, if product cost reduction programs should achieve only 70 percent of target, what pricing actions might be taken? If an over-supplied product pipeline should empty more slowly than predicted, what shifts in marketing expenditures would be appropriate?

One way to deal with contingencies is to develop strategies and action plans to be activated when a key performance or environ-mental variable drops to a certain level.[3] The objective is to neu-tralize or offset the adverse consequences as much as possible. Some strategies need to be executed in advance as *insurance*, per-haps by stockpiling critical materials in anticipation of transportation problems. Other strategies, such as layoffs, delays, or cost contain-ment programs, will be ready to put into action when they are needed. Thus, contingency plans must also specify a *trigger point* or warning signal of the imminence of the event for which the action plans are designed. This puts a premium on careful monitoring of critical trends and on a willingness to move quickly when the criti-cal event is about to occur. Having the contingency plans on the shelf decreases the likelihood of an emotional shortterm response that might threaten the base strategy.

Formal contingency plans sound good on paper, but in practice their value is questionable. As one NASA veteran of many space launches observed, "It's the unanticipated risks that really matter." The real value of contingency thinking seems to come from consid-ering changes in strategy that would reduce either the probability of an adverse event occuring or the impact of the event when it does

---

3. Procedures for developing these plans are described in detail in O'Connor (1978).

happen. For example, if the business is judged vulnerable to the loss of a major customer who is getting close to having sufficient volume to backward integrate, then action steps such as more aggressive pricing or enhancing the value of the product are suggested.

The Survival Question Technique.   This technique is an extension of contingency analysis in which management identifies environmental conditions that would threaten the survival of the company or business. The heart of the technique [4] is the generation of a lengthy list of "candidate survival questions" in the form of "Can business or product XYZ survive if . . . ?" The question is completed with a projection of a potential development in the external environment, such as

> . . . a large part of Middle East oil is cut off for an extended period?
>
> . . . U.S. interest rates substantially exceed inflation rates for the next several years?
>
> . . . we lose our major account?

While 50 to 100 such questions are usually generated, the answer to most is yes, leaving only a few areas where survival is definitely in doubt. If the likelihood is significant that the environmental event will occur, the company or business must then set an objective to survive that environment and to develop the appropriate strategies.

An early user of this technique was Citicorp. One candidate survival question asked if Citicorp would survive if the world monetary system should collapse. As this possibility was judged to be significant during the 1980s, the question demanded attention. Citicorp concluded that they should not only restructure their business to survive but also do what they could to avert a collapse.

A variant of this technique asks what the business has to do to break even if volume drops by 10 percent, 20 percent, or 30 percent. This question serves to identify opportunities for reducing overhead and fixed costs. Indeed, this became the basis for a "survival plan" that many businesses developed during the sharp 1982 recession so they could be better prepared to deal with a serious downturn.

---

4. Frederick (1982).

Resolve Key Issues

One of the most useful outputs of the situation assessment is a consensus among operating managers on the key issues to be resolved. Issues are framed, using the steps laid out in Chapter 3, as questions requiring intense analysis and task force studies that yield specific options.

Such an issues resolution study was initiated by a medium-sized security systems company following the assessment of one of their major businesses. As part of the planning process, each of six product market segments was positioned in a market attractiveness and competitive strength matrix. Relative to other businesses, this was clearly a stable "manage for current earnings" situation. Yet, the cash flow consequences of the current strategy were wildly at variance with this strategic thrust. The problem was eventually traced to the need to carry substantial finished goods inventories to satisfy the distributors of one product line. This situation had been obscured by limitations of the accounting system and an unusual one-time improvement in cash generated by the business during the previous year. Many options were considered for dealing with the issue, including dropping the product line, revamping the entire distribution system, streamlining inventory management, or a combination of these. An impressive amount of creativity was unleashed in response to this pressing and specific problem.

Issues often demand separate attention simply because they do not conform to the planning calendar. They may move too quickly to permit timely perception and response within the planning cycle, or may occur between cycles. Indeed, when a business has established a clear and relatively stable strategic direction that takes several years to execute—but operates in a turbulent environment—an annual plan is a waste of time. Worse, it may become a routine exercise that merely elaborates an existing budgeting process. Until a significant change occurs in the premises underlying the current direction, directing attention to dealing with emerging issues is a better approach.

Find Analogies

Challenges to the present strategy are understandably constrained by an innate reluctance to step beyond the familiar bounds of the present strategy. Contributing to this reluctance is the limited array of strategies that most managers have directly experienced. One way to expand this narrow experience base is to consciously identify analogous situations and the characteristics of successful strategies in these situations.

A good starting point is the experience of winners in similar industries in the same geographic region or country. This approach was used by Hall [5] in a study of the two top performers in eight basic industries with hostile operating environments. Average profitability in industries such as tires, steel, and heavy-duty trucks was low, as would be expected in light of their capital intensity, foreign competition, and maturity. Yet, the survivors in these industries reported profits in the top 20 percent of the Fortune 1000 industrials. Hall concluded that the outstanding performance of these companies was due to "continuous, single-minded determination" to achieve either or both the lowest delivered cost position and the highest product/service/quality differentiated position relative to competition, coupled with both an acceptable delivered cost structure and a pricing policy to gain margins sufficient to fund reinvestment in product/service differentiation.

Multinational firms often have explicit procedures to ensure that the results of successful strategy experiments in one country are transferred to other operating companies with similar environments. National companies can also adapt this approach. An Australian shoe company with serious distribution problems in one region of the country carefully studied the distribution systems used by similar companies in European countries for strategies they could adapt.

Another source of useful analogies is *precursors*. These could be geographic areas, such as California, that have previously signaled changes in buying trends and competitive activity that presented threats or opportunities. For the same reason, Canadian financial service companies are closely studying the experience of their counterparts in the United States, who have had several more years to adapt to deregulation.

A logical extension of this line of thinking is the PIMS program. The core of this program is a data base, summarizing the strategic experience of 2,200 businesses over as long a period as ten years. This data base can be used to answer the question, What has been the experience of "strategy peers" who have conducted a series of strategy experiments from similar competitive positions and with similar resources?

---

5. Hall (1980).

Look for Strategic Windows

A strategic window is "open" when the fit between the critical success factors in a market and the distinctive competencies of a business serving that market is at an optimum. The period during which a strategic window exists and can be exploited by a firm may be quite short. Windows close when the resource requirements for success change dramatically, for the competencies of a business can seldom be adjusted so rapidly. The change in key success factors not only has to be recognized and the implications correctly interpreted, but also the business has to overcome strong emotional, financial, and physical ties to the skills[6] and resources that have worked so well in the past. Sometimes, obtaining the new requirements for successful competition is simply not possible.

The challenge for businesses already serving the market is to cope with the changes that threaten the position of the firm. For example, wristwatches used to be differentiated by accuracy that was a consequence of the manufacturing technology. In the wake of mass-produced large-scale integrated (LSI) chips and frequency oscillators, however, accuracy is no longer a distinguishing factor. Differentiation is now based on such factors as functional features or elegance and fashion appeal. For existing watchmakers or, indeed, any firm facing such a dramatic shift in resource requirements, the options are:

- to attempt to assemble the resources needed to close the gap between the new requirements and the existing competencies,
- to focus on selected segments in which the fit is still acceptable,
- to harvest or exit the business.

For potential entrants, an open strategic window is a significant opportunity to be grasped quickly. The window often results from the application of a technology developed in one market to an opportunity in another. Most firms presently serving a market have a limited capability to master all the technologies that might ultimately cannibalize their business. Control over technology, however, is not a sufficient condition for success unless it corresponds to a critical success factor. Indeed, Ohmae[7] argues that the most effec-

---

6. Abell (1978).
7. Ohmae (1982).

tive shortcut to a leadership position is an early concentration of major resources on a single strategically significant function in order to excel in that area, and then a consolidation of the lead in the other functions.

The message underlying these responses to a strategic window is that successful strategies come from simultaneously building on competencies and exploiting environmental opportunities.

Capitalize on Environmental Trends.   Critical success factors can change as a result of almost any trend or discontinuity in the environment. Major pressures for change, however, tend to come from the following sources:

- *market* evolution, creating new primary demand opportunities with different requirements, or changing the segmentation structure,

- *technological* evolution, which changes the nature of the market if new functions are provided and may create an entirely new class of competitors,

- changes in the *value-added* system as customers, competitors, or suppliers vertically integrate and combine stages or create new stages.

These sources of change often interact in complex patterns to create strategic windows. For example, Firestone is undertaking a major expansion of its auto service business by capitalizing on two major changes in the market.[8] First, many gas stations, squeezed for profits during the oil shortages of the seventies, have been closed. Second, auto dealers with repair facilities were hard hit by the 1982 recession and were frequently forced to close. Consequently, in 1983 there were 30 percent fewer service bays in the United States than there were ten years ago. At the same time, car owners were keeping their cars longer and spending more money on service to keep them running. Firestone would have had difficulty capitalizing on these trends, had developments in computer analyzers for diagnosing engine problems not been available to help overcome a lack of competency in auto engine repair. Until recently, most of Firestone's repair work involved parts related to tire wear, such as shock absorbers and brakes. They can now be reasonably confident of doing satisfactory repairs on more complex systems and of overcoming the consumer perception that they are competent only in selling and maintaining tires.

---

8. "Firestone Tries the Service Business Again." *Business Week* (20 June 1983).

Many windows are opened—and closed—during the transition to market maturity and the resulting shift in buyer requirements. One of the ironies of maturity is that "the more a seller expands the market by teaching and helping customers to use his product, the more vulnerable he becomes to losing them. When a customer no longer needs help, he gains the flexibility to shop for things he values more—such as price."[9] Since not all buyers change the market becomes fragmented into more segments. Some segments become very price sensitive, while others require augmented benefits beyond the minimum performance level. Few firms can effectively compete to satisfy both these requirements. Many of these patterns of evolution can be analyzed within the context of technological and product life cycles, which are discussed in depth in a companion volume in this series.

Building on Competencies.   As we emphasized in Chapter 3, the relative balance of strengths or distinctive competencies versus weaknesses determines the ability to succeed in a changing environment. Competencies, however, are not static; they must constantly be nourished, adapted, and reinforced to be effective. The response of American Airlines to the deregulation of airlines that began in 1978 is illustrative of the strategy of building on competencies. The problem was to distinguish the airline from other trunk carriers as well as from the new low-cost, point-to-point competitors. The elements of the strategy were (1) a refocusing on the frequent flier segment that was their original constituency, (2) a transformation of a largely linear system into a hub-and-spoke network, (3) a reinforcement of the strong service tradition by adherence to high service standards despite higher labor costs, and (4) exploitation of their computer systems capabilities. By an early recognition of the need for these computer systems, American took the lead in the computerized reservation systems that travel agents buy or lease from airlines. As a result, in 1982 their Sabre system was used by 41 percent of computerized travel agencies. The immediate significance of this coverage lies in the fact that the system supplier can influence an agent by putting its flights in preferred positions on the screen that displays all the flights that could satisfy a requested departure and arrival schedule. The customer record-keeping capabilities of the Sabre system have also been the basis for programs to build brand loyalty. Frequent fliers are rewarded for mileage

---

9. Levitt (1980).

flown with free trips and free upgrades to first class. By building on these competencies, American has also achieved a competitive advantage. This advantage will be sustainable so long as the travel agents remain satisfied with the service and other airlines are unwilling to make the investment to replace it.

Redefine the Business

A strategic window is a precipitating event that requires both incumbents and potential entrants to rethink the scope of their business definitions. We can be confident only that "business as usual" will not be an appropriate strategic response.

Consider the boxed example [10] which illustrates the need for a business redefinition.

A medium-sized manufacturer of passive electronics components (such as resistors, capacitors, and inductors) was facing a major revolution due to rapid developments in integrated circuits (ICs). These ICs were expected to profoundly affect the design, cost, and performance of all electronics equipment, including the passive components they used.

The signals of impending change came from the sales force, customers, and a captive IC division in another part of the corporation. It was clear that many passive components would be eliminated. Those that were used would have to be smaller and lighter, carry less power, and be more precise than current products.

Some segments of the passive components market were expected to grow, however, because ICs could not perform such critical functions as inductance, capacitance, high or precise resistance, circuit trimming, or tuning and interconnection.

The recognition of these changes led to a redefinition of the business as a supplier of passive components/packages/connectors that are compatible with ICs used by electronics equipment manufacturers. In support of this redefinition, a number of strategic options were considered including the addition of new products by acquisition, licensing or internal development. These would be sold through the present sales force and distribution system. Ten major growth markets were identified, including precision resistors, tantalum and electrolytic resistors, sensors, and potentiometers. Over an eight-year period, three major business segments were added, each contributing significantly to a growth in sales and profits of 20 percent per year.

---

10. Adapted from C. Davis Fogg (1983).

The strategic implication of a business redefinition can greatly be clarified by forcing one's thinking along each dimension of the business definition and asking such questions as:

- Are the categories along each of the dimensions—which describe alternative functions, technologies, value-added stages, or segments—still relevant? Perhaps narrower segment groups are emerging, functions are being combined, or existing technologies offer the possibility of providing new functions.

- What alternative positions within the current business scope should be considered? For example, Holiday Inns is giving greater priority to upscale business travelers who travel frequently and who will pay for specialized services. The challenge is to overcome the image of Holiday Inns as a provider of middle-value roadside hotel rooms.

- What related categories of function, segment, or technology presently outside the business definition could be served? Insights into this latter question can come from examining trends in the market, as well as functions and segments that are part of the business definition of competitors.

Each of these questions suggests a possible strategic option—or element of a change in strategy—that can further be developed and evaluated.

Play on Competitors' Vulnerabilities

Firms that have identified a strategic window must consider the response of competitors when deciding which competency to emphasize and how the competency should be used to advantage. In this search for competitive advantage, the guiding principle is to *concentrate strength against the competitiors' relative weakness.* The goal is to dissuade competitors from reacting by eliminating their ability or willingness to respond. The military rationale was provided by Liddell Hart:[11]

We can at least crystallize the lessons into two simple maxims.
    . . . The first is that, in the face of the overwhelming evidence

---

11. Liddell Hart (1967).

of history, no general is justified in launching his troops in a direct attack upon an enemy firmly in position. The second, that instead of seeking to upset the enemy's equilibrium by one's attack, it must be upset before a real attack is, or can be, successfully launched.

Two complementary approaches for devising a strategy of indirect attacks are to sidestep or negate barriers to entry, and then to influence the competitors' perception of the strategy.

Avoiding Entry Barriers

When a business enters an existing market, it encounters barriers that exact a cost from all entrants crossing them. Five major barriers must be overcome if the direct entry is to be successful:

- cost disadvantages (due to scale economies, experience, or unique factor costs)
- product differentiation
- capital requirements
- switching costs
- access to distribution channels

These entry barriers are the source of the cost/investment discontinuities that were discussed in Chapter 4 as a basis for identifying market boundaries.

Each of the costs imposed by an entry barrier is likely to be accentuated if the entrant follows the same strategy as existing competitors: matching product for product, price for price, and promotion for promotion. This is an invitation to retaliation, with the outcome depending on who has greater resources, commitment, and endurance. Kodak's experience in the instant photography market illustrates the hazards of a frontal challenge to an established competitor.[12] Kodak entered with a Kodamatic instant camera, which was judged to be a Polaroid clone, against a company that was deeply and emotionally committed to retaining its leadership position. Indeed, Polaroid's entire identity was wrapped up in this market. To maintain their position, Polaroid unleashed deep price cuts, new product features, and aggressive promotional programs. At great expense, they were able to stall Kodak's entry and hold it to a 35 percent market share. Analysts doubt that the Kodamatic

---

12. Moore (1983).

has made any money for the company since it was launched in 1976.

As an alternative to a direct frontal attack, the new entrant may use a modified version of the incumbent's strategy, such as making a significant price cut, while matching other aspects of the offer. This can work if the leading competitors do not match the price cut (usually because too many gross margin dollars are at stake) and the customers can be persuaded that the new entrant's product is of acceptable quality. This strategy has successfully been used by Helene Curtis—producing budget imitations of leading high-priced brands of health-care and beauty-aid products such as shampoos. They promote them with blatant comparative advertisements that say, "We do what theirs does for less than half the price."[13]

Flanking Attacks.[14]   The drawbacks of a direct confrontation are compelling arguments for strategies that seek to avoid retaliation. The most successful of these flanking strategies have two characteristics in common with the effective market penetration strategies described in the previous chapter:

1. The new entrant appeals to a previously unserved or unsatisfied segment that has the potential to be developed into a strong segment. Consumer goods companies have prospered by entering fast-growing age segments and meeting their needs. (At present, the thirty to forty-five age category is the fastest growing demographic segment, and consumers start to worry about looking old when they enter that age segment.) Similarly, the Hispanic market offers long-term potential for specialty foods, as the ethnic group is not only the fastest growing in the United States but also maintains a distinct culture.

2. The incumbents are likely to be restrained from immediate retaliation by matching the entrant's product because of concerns over cannibalization of existing sales or a fear of giving the entrant a seal of approval.

Both these conditions characterized Toshiba's successful entry into the CT (computerized tomography) scanner market. They first identified a segment of doctors that did not want all the sophisticat-

---

13. Further examples of modified frontal attack can be found in Kotler and Singh Achrol (1981).

14. Yip (1982).

ed features of scanners designed for use in large hospitals, and offered a stripped-down version. The incumbents, General Electric and Siemens, found it difficult to respond to this challenge because of negative impacts on the rest of their product line. The Toshiba example points up a further feature of successful flanking attacks—the conscious effort to design products and manufacturing processes to surmount cost, capital, and differentiation barriers. This was also done by Versatec in their entry into the low end of the computer plotter market with a standardized, modular machine and a minimum scale of operations.

A flank position also provides a base to gain experience and credibility as a prelude to an entry into the larger core market. This was the route that Michelin followed with steel-belted radial tires to gain access to the U.S. tire market.

Influencing Competitors' Decisions

Indirect strategies rely on the incumbents' responses being restrained by their own commitments. Further restraints can be introduced by manipulating these competitors' perceptions of the situation. Henderson [15] offers several types of strategic moves to serve this end:

1. Appear to be unworthy of attention. Quickly cut off a part of the market that is too small to justify a major response. Repeat.

2. Appear to be unbeatable. Convince competitors that if they follow your lead or practices, they will gain nothing since you will equal or better any market actions they take.

3. Avoid attention. Be secretive. Do not let competitors know about new products, policies or capabilities until it is too late for them to respond effectively.

4. Redirect attention. Focus competitive attention on the major volume areas of company sales, not on the high potential areas.

The key to strategies based on competitors' responses is an understanding of their strengths and weaknesses as well as their willingness to act and react competitively. Simply finding and acting on a competitor's weakness is an insufficient basis for achieving an advantage. If they have the same information, they may well

---

15. Henderson (1979).

anticipate and correct their problems, and thus may thwart your strategic initiative. Only if competitors are put in a position in which they cannot win by retaliating will they be likely to avoid conflict. To assess this point, however, it is essential to be able to view the world from competitors' eyes as well as from your own.

Change the Rules of the Competitive Game

California home builders tend to think of their customer base as the traditional nuclear family, and usually rely on developers or real estate agents to do their selling. These assumptions about appropriate strategies are being rudely shaken by the British home builder, Barratt Developments PLC.[16] They are changing the rules of the competitive game in three areas:

- Market segmentation. Barratt segments the market much more finely than California home builders, and then designs homes to meet the specific needs of distinct groups. For example, they design a 600 square foot apartment for retirees whose children have long since left home. The developments, however, are equipped with common rooms for entertaining and with spare apartments for visitors.

- Direct selling. Shoppers in several Sears, Roebuck stores can now find full-scale, fully furnished condominiums for sale right in the store.

- Low prices for a complete housing package. The price tag for a Barratt home is half the going rate for a new home in California. The price can include the complete furnishings and all necessary mortgage financing to provide a simple package for one-step buying. The company also accepts trade-ins on old homes.

The basis for Barratt's strategy is a challenge to both conventional wisdom—which limits the actions of existing competitors—and the structural forces that bear heavily on the profitability of the industry. These challenges, singly or together, are a fertile source of strategic options to both incumbents and new entrants.

---

16. "A British Builder Exports Its Blueprint for Affordable Homes." *Business Week* (18 July 1983).

Challenge the Conventional Wisdom

The widespread, uncritical acceptance of the conventional wisdom is precisely what makes it so difficult to challenge. Even if one has grown up within an industry and has absorbed all the unwritten rules and assumptions, articulating the conventional wisdom may still be difficult. Outsiders often see more clearly the potential for strategic change that is inherent in these unquestioned assumptions.

One framework for summarizing the conventional wisdom about competitive strategies is the competitive advantage matrix.[17] The feasible strategy thrusts in a market are shaped by the number of unique ways that advantage can be obtained, and the size of the advantage that can be created, over other competitors. The underlying logic is that the profitability and long-run value of the business is directly related to the opportunity to create an advantage. Where the advantage is small, the returns of the entire industry will be depressed. Four possible strategic thrusts are suggested by the ubiquitous four-cell matrix created by combining these two dimensions, as shown in Figure 6.1.

Each cell in Figure 6.1 describes a characteristic industry environment that dictates some general strategy prescriptions. For example, in *volume* industries, in which there are only a few ways to achieve advantages that are potentially large, one of the strategies is often to cut costs by increasing volume. If a business has such an advantage in this type of industry, it should attack the weakest competitors by aggressively cutting prices and gaining additional volume.

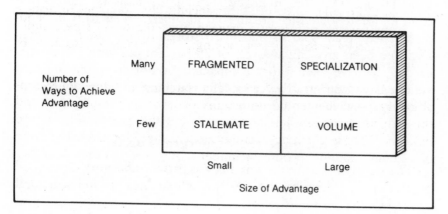

Figure 6.1 The Competitive Advantage Matrix

17. Lochridge (1981).

In *specialization* industries, in which the business has opportunities for improvements on many fronts and may have achieved advantage on one or more, the indicated strategy is to maintain one's position and prevent competitors from achieving the same type of advantage. The Japanese are believed to have used this strategy in invading the U.S. auto market with high-quality, gas-efficient compacts.

Within *fragmented* industries such as restaurants, a competitor can distinguish itself from others in many ways, but none of them help much. Here, the indicated strategy is to minimize investment, try to get returns up, hold position, and expand cautiously.

Most of the time the matrix probably defines the feasible options correctly. But it can also be a trap if the implicit assumptions are internalized too quickly and accepted as conventional wisdom. The constraints on thinking imposed by premature acceptance of the rules of the competitive game derived from this matrix are illustrated by the prescriptions for *stalemated* industries such as paper or steel. The indicated strategy—when there are few ways to achieve advantage—is to conserve cash, find new opportunities, and exit if possible. This would seem to be the advice that has been followed in the ice cream market, in which the number of competitors has declined from 2,000 to 350 in the past twenty years.[18] Because transportation costs are high, most ice cream is produced within a 500-mile radius of where it is consumed. To keep prices down, manufacturers have whipped air into the product and have added chemical stabilizers and artificial flavors and colors. Just because the industry behaved as though it were stalemated, however, did not mean that the rules of the game could not be changed. This is what Haagen-Dazs has done by shifting the basis of competition from undifferentiated ice cream sold in supermarkets to rich, hand-packed ice cream sold in franchised stores. As a result, Haagen-Dazs has been growing at a rate of 25 percent per year. They succeeded, as have many other companies, by not accepting the conventional wisdom and by creatively searching for new sources of advantage that they could dominate.

Challenge the Structural Forces

The departure point for this analysis is the framework developed by Porter [19] to describe the five forces that bear on the structural profitability of an industry:

---

18. Pekar (1982)
19. Porter (1980).

- rivalry among existing competitors
- bargaining power of suppliers
- bargaining power of buyers
- threat of substitutes
- threat of new entrants

Once these forces are understood, the question for strategy developers is how to neutralize those forces that are depressing profitability. The approach that Jordache has taken in the U.S. blue jeans industry is illustrative of what can be done.

In the mid-1970's industry profits were low except for Levi Strauss and, Blue Bell, maker of Wrangler jeans. Low-entry barriers had allowed almost 100 small manufacturers to enter the blue jeans market. All they needed was some equipment, relatively low-skilled labor, and an empty warehouse. These small manufacturers had little influence over raw materials pricing. The production of denim was concentrated in the hands of four textile companies. At the same time, the sales of jeans were concentrated in a few major store chains with significant bargaining power.

Jordache was able to change these industry forces by creating designer jeans and by supporting them with heavy advertising. This lowered the bargaining power of the major chains by creating strong consumer preferences. As a result, the chains had to accept Jordache's prices. Also, the strategy created significant new-entry barriers. Even though its products were imitated, the field of competitors in the designer jeans segment is significantly smaller than in the commodity segment, and price pressures are less severe.

The end purpose of these moves is to gain a sustainable competitive advantage. Whereas these moves are based on superior understanding of competitors' capabilities and willingness to respond, another approach is to achieve advantage through superior understanding of the present and potential customers. Ideally, both perspectives should be employed simultaneously.

Enhance Customer Value

The ability to offer target customer segments superior value, even at a higher price, provides a distinctive—and hard to match—competitive advantage. Here, value means the subjective judgment by the customer of the worth and desirability of the product or service in the usage situation. The context of the judgment of value is often much broader than the initial cost. Thus, a manufacturer of computer printers that significantly upgraded quality was able to reduce the lifetime service cost of its printers from $2,500 to $500 on average. Even though the initial price was increased from $4,000 to $5,000, the overall value was greatly enhanced, and the market share quadrupled.

The concept of *relative value in use* (RVU) provides a useful framework for analyzing the value provided by current offerings and for suggesting strategies for enhancing competitive advantage.[20] RVU is defined as the maximum amount a customer should be willing to pay for the firm's product, assuming he or she is fully informed about the firm's product and the offerings of the competitors. The reference point for this analysis is the life cycle cost of the closest competitive alternative. This reference product need not be a physically similar product; it can be any product that fulfills the function or need. The RVU will differ from the purchase price of this reference product by the amount of perceived *savings* in start-up and postpurchase costs, and any *augmented value* that the firm's product provides (see Figure 6.2). The analysis of relative value is undertaken within each usage situation or application, for differences in RVU result from the ways customers use and derive value from their respective reference products. For example, the

Figure 6.2 Customer Value Analysis Estimated for Each Usage Situation

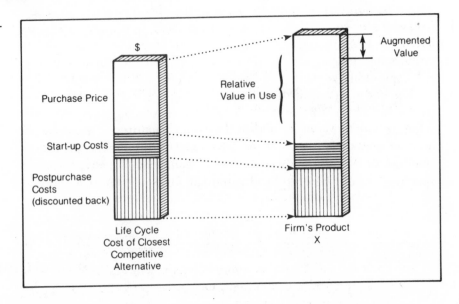

20. RVU is very similar to the notion of economic value to the customer developed by Forbis and Mehta (1982).

RVU of a minicomputer will depend on whether it is being compared with other mini- or microcomputers, and on whether it is used for a production line control, distributed processing, or energy saving application.

An analysis of relative value in use is particularly revealing when the product delivers a stream of benefits or value over time, and when tangible or intangible attributes can be added to augment the value. One such attribute is *usefulness:* a product may supplement or magnify a human effort, save time, or provide a new function. This was the route Intel followed in the mid-seventies in a situation that required that microprocessors be tailored to specific applications. They developed a general purpose microprocessor that could easily be programmed to fit many applications. This development not only saved customers considerable design and manufacturing time but also improved reliability. At the same time, Intel achieved economies of scale in mass production. Other attributes that can be used to augment value are *security* (the intangible benefits of safety and protection and the tangible benefits of reduced downtime from greater reliability) and *availability* (customers will pay a premium for immediate delivery on the assurance of low stock levels).

Enhancing Competitive Advantage. A knowledge of the currently perceived relative values and segment variations in RVU suggests a number of directions in which to look for opportunities to gain a competitive advantage:

- design or technology changes (or both) to reduce life cycle costs. This usually requires a choice between a reduction in initial versus operating costs.

- augment value by adding functional features. These can be designed to increase the user's capacity, help the user to improve the quality or reliability of his end product, or enhance end-product flexibility. Thus, boilers that can easily burn a number of alternative fuels offer a significant benefit to customers facing uncertain energy supplies.

- augment value through incorporation of superior performance on intangibles such as service, financing, or delivery. For example, heavy equipment manufacturers can gain an advantage among small contractors by providing strong local service and low-cost financing options.

In practice, customers will not switch from their existing suppliers unless the inducement is substantial. Setting a price that is marginal-

ly below the RVU is not sufficient, for this will not overcome iner-
tia, uncertainty about the long-term benefits, or reluctance to
change suppliers. Even more inducement is required if the customer does not accurately perceive the relative benefits and understates
the RVU. This also indicates a need for a carefully directed communications program and a well-trained sales force in close contact
with key decision makers to influence the comparative evaluations
of suppliers.

Summary

This chapter builds on the insights gained during the situation
assessment phase of the process to creatively generate strategic
options for the business. Within the broad framework suggested
by the portfolio position and generic strategy options, the real
insights come from a systematic process of challenging the present
strategy and focusing on the fundamental factors of competitive
advantage, key success factors, and relative customer value. This
puts a premium on a thorough understanding of the capabilities of
the business and its competitors and opportunities in the market
environment.

Each of these approaches and the supporting concepts serves as a
stimulus to thinking, but does not provide a ready-made answer.
Ultimately, the feasible options to be evaluated in the next chapter
have to be grounded in the reality of the specific situation:

> The secret lies in making people think from the very start, What can
> we do? instead of What can't we do? and then striving doggedly
> to strip away one by one the constraints that have turned the possi-
> ble into the seemingly impossible.[21]

---

21. Ohmae (1982).

Evaluating the Strategic Options

Chapter 7

Strategic decisions appear—after the fact—to emerge from a neat, linear process of narrowing a wide range of possible options until a clear-cut choice is made. The reality seldom bears much resemblance to this idealized view. What is generally experienced is a lengthy and circuitous process, during which some options are rejected early (and perhaps even prematurely), new options are formed by combining the best features of several options, and refinements and details are continually being added. The choice of one from among several viable options is equally torturous, involving difficult trade-offs among conflicting objectives amid considerable uncertainty.

Coping with this complexity requires explicit, widely understood criteria to guide the various stages of evaluation and selection of options. The primary purpose of this chapter is to provide a robust set of criteria that have proven useful in a variety of business situations. In discussing the use of these criteria in practice, we have to be sensitive to the pitfalls and biases that are likely to be encountered. Several suggestions are offered for dealing with these problems, including a procedure for surfacing and testing the critical assumptions that underlie judgments about specific strategy options.

> *A decision is a judgment. It is a choice between alternatives. It is rarely a choice between right and wrong. It is at best a choice between "almost right" and "probably wrong"—but much more often a choice between two courses of action neither of which is provably more nearly right than the other.*
>
> *—Peter Drucker*

Criteria for Evaluating Strategy Options

The evaluation of a strategy is much like the testing of a scientific theory. While a theory can never be shown to be absolutely true, it can be declared absolutely false if it fails to stand up to testing. Similarly, it is impossible to be assured that a strategy is optimal or to even guarantee it will work. What is needed are evaluative criteria that can be used to isolate critical flaws and to increase the odds that the best option will be chosen from the set. Each of the following criteria can also be used to systematically seek areas for improvement in the strategy under review:

- *Suitability.* Is the proposed strategy consistent with the foreseeable environmental threats and opportunities? Does the strategy exploit or enhance a current competitive advantage, or create a new source of advantage?

- *Validity.* Are the key assumptions about environmental trends and the outcomes of the strategy realistic? Are the assumptions based on reliable and valid information?

- *Consistency.* Are the basic elements of the strategy consistent with each other and with the objectives being pursued?

- *Feasibility.* Is the strategy appropriate to the available resources? Are the basic elements and premises of the strategy understandable and acceptable to the operating managers who will have the responsibility for implementation?

- *Vulnerability.* To what extent are projected outcomes dependent on data or assumptions of dubious quality and origin? Are the risks of failure acceptable? Are there adequate contingency plans for coping with these risks? Can the decision be reversed in the future? How long will it take? What are the consequences?

- *Potential rewards.* Are the projected outcomes satisfactory in light of the provisional objectives for the business? Are the adjustments to the objectives acceptable to the stakeholders?

These criteria play an important role in shaping the direction of the business by setting the standards to be met before action plans can be formulated. In the remainder of this section, we will review the individual criteria in depth.

Suitability:
Is There a Sustainable Advantage?

The essence of strategy formulation is the matching of competencies with threats and opportunities. Hence, an important first question is whether the strategic option makes sense in light of anticipated changes in the external environment. For example, until the early eighties, "systems houses" dominated the market for turnkey computer systems. These firms prospered by offering a total solution to a customer's problems by providing both applications software and computer hardware. The market growth of packaged systems, of 40 percent per year, unfortunately attracted the attention of hardware manufacturers. Faced with rapidly declining hardware prices, these new competitors were beginning to emphasize software. Thus, any strategy option had to recognize the impact of much larger, better-funded, and highly visible hardware makers and computer service companies.

Strategy, however, is also about the pursuit of competitive advantage. If no basis exists for future competitive advantage or for adaptation to the forces eroding the current competitive advantage, then the strategy does not stand the test. By mid-1980, it was apparent that systems houses that continued to emphasize general business applications such as accounting and payroll were most vulnerable, because the expertise was not great.[1] By contrast, systems houses with specializations in technically complex markets—chromatography systems, for example—and the capability to provide a range of products, including remote data processing and systems consulting, had a protected advantage and attractive growth prospects.

A number of steps should be followed when subjecting each strategy option to the suitability test:

Step One: Review the potential threats and opportunities to the business from

- changes in the environment, especially from changes in customer and distribution requirements,
- the actions of present and prospective competitors,
- changes in the availability of critical skills and resources.

Step Two: Assess each option in light of capacity to

- ward off or avoid threats,
- exploit opportunities, and
- enhance current advantages or provide new sources of advantage.

At this stage it is worth asking whether the strategy can work under a broad range of foreseeable environment conditions. Some strategies are only effective when inflation is high, or low, for example. Other strategies don't travel well, and are not suitable in all product-markets. A robust strategy, that can be readily adapted to a

---

1. "New Rivals in Turnkey Systems." *Business Week* (23 June 1980).

variety of conditions is much preferred, for frequent changes are not only costly but they disorient the organization and the market.

Step Three: Anticipate the likely competitive responses to each option. Can competitors match, offset, or leapfrog any advantages conferred by this option? Here, role playing by management teams taking the perspectives of different competitors can be valuable. To complete this step, the option should be tested by asking how the business would cope with the anticipated competitive actions.

Step Four: If the strategy option does not meet these suitability tests, it should be either modified or dropped from further consideration. Hence, this is a major screening test.

The boxed insert on page 156 describes a strategy that did not satisfy this pivotal criterion.

Validity:
Are the Assumptions Realistic?

Choices among competing strategic options are among the most ambiguous and least structured of all decisions that managers must make. "For this kind of choice the executive has little hard data to go on. Rather he must construct his own reality from the raw material at his disposal. Reality construction involves the utmost in uncertainty and at the bottom of this web of strategic uncertainty lie assumptions." [2] Furthermore, all those with a stake in choosing and implementing the strategy must share those assumptions. Otherwise, the strategy will be formulated through compromise and will be implemented without understanding or conviction.

The difficulty lies in distinguishing sound from faulty assumptions. One must constantly be on guard for assumptions that are widely accepted as conventional wisdom but have never been thoughtfully examined, or for those that cannot be justified in light of past events or probable trends. Indeed, whenever a major departure from past performance is anticipated, it is important to test whether adequate basis exists for the forecast. Table 7.1 shows how this was done in the case of a proposed strategy for an industrial components business that forecast an increase of $51 million in sales and $7 million in net income between 1983 and 1987.

---

2. Mason and Mitroff (1981).

Table 7.1 Testing Key Strategic Assumptions

SOURCES OF CHANGE	1983–1987 ($MM)		KEY ASSUMPTIONS/ ACTIONS	VALIDITY
	SALES	NET INCOME		
TOTAL CHANGE	51	7		
■ Price Increase	23	12	■ 8.5% yearly increase (inflation rate = 9%)	■ 1981 = 7.6% 1982 = 5.3% ■ industry 80% capacity and Japanese threat ■ growing share simultaneously
■ Share Improvement	17	4	■ 31% to 34% in industrial segment ■ 20% to 27% in commercial segment	■ increase 0.6%/year 1978–79 but with minimal price increase ■ industrial segment is a high-price sensitivity market ■ new products in commercial segment are catch-up
■ Real Market Growth	10	2	■ 7% per year	■ 2% yearly, 1980–82 ■ 20% from unproven new market X
COST				
■ Productivity	1	1	■ 3% per year	■ 70% of annual 3%/year 1978–82 improvement was a single technical process breakthrough
■ Compensation Increase		(12)	■ head count up 24%	■ head count 1983 same as 1980 with 10% less volume

A Failure in Strategy Evaluation

Recently, Greyhound and Trailways took on one another in a fierce and profitless strategic maneuver over passenger bus fares. Greyhound, in an effort to boost passenger traffic on its intercity bus routes, in early 1978 announced a $50 fare applying to all trips extending more than 1,000 miles. Trailways responded with a series of commercials on national television proclaiming the cheapest rates from New York to Los Angeles.

However, the promotional war drew in little new business, mainly because it took no account of the changing market for intercity bus service. The reduced fares were aimed at long-distance travellers—despite the fact that fewer than 5 percent of all bus passengers ride 1,000 miles or more. Most of the passenger market for distances over 500 miles is captured by the airlines. Even though air fares are roughly 50 percent higher than bus fares, the travel time is much less on long trips. For instance, at the height of the Greyhound-Trailways price war, the lowest one-way bus fare from Chicago to Miami was $69 and involved travel time of a day and a half; by airplane the fare was $99 and flight time was two and one half hours—a comparison which pinpoints the strategic folly of the bus lines' attempt to attract long-distance business.

At the same time, both Trailways and Greyhound failed to focus their business strategy on the short-haul market of less than 200 miles, the segment containing 40 percent of all intercity travel. Moreover, they ignored the airlines' long-standing and successful strategy of structuring their routes into networks of short-haul markets, where each major city serves as the hub for a series of spokes or corridor routes radiating out for 100–200 miles to smaller cities and other key hubs. Instead, buses were often run on a continuing schedule from one end of the country to the other, passing through many metropolitan areas in the middle of the night and not during prime-time travel hour.

Source: Loving (1978).

The first step in the validity test is to isolate each of the assumptions about the reasons for the forecast changes. For example, sales and profits are expected to benefit from a combination of price increases close to the rate of inflation, real market growth of 7 percent per year in the forecast period, and substantial share gains in both market segments. The next step is to evaluate the evidence used to support each assumption. Here, the basis for the assumptions about share gains and real market growth appears especially tenuous. How can any share gains be realistically justified when the new products in the commercial segment do not appear to offer a competitive advantage, and the business is trying to hold prices in the industrial segment close to inflation while countering potential Japanese competition? On the evidence, one has little confidence the proposed strategy could deliver the promised results. New evidence has to be provided and the forecasts adjusted to fit market realities and to reflect trade-offs between conflicting performance objectives.

Finally, all assumptions rely on information that itself may be inaccurate, misleading, or simply out of date. Thus, it is important to continually ask how the data were collected, by whom, and for what purpose. These questions apply equally to internally generated data on costs or salespersons' calling frequency or coverage, and environmental data on growth, market size, and price levels. Information on changes in competitors' capabilities and customer requirements must be scrutinized with special care. The consequences of not doing so were graphically described by the president of the Becton-Dickinson Consumer Products Group in 1980 as he reflected on their experience with strategic planning:

> Four years ago I went through a planning session with the Diabetic Care SBU, which makes, among other products, the syringes diabetics use to give themselves insulin. We had an excellent profiling session, and the strategy we developed seemed like a perfect one.
>
> During the next year we suffered a serious loss of market share.
>
> What happened was that a competitor introduced a syringe with a finer-gauged needle. We had known the competitor's plans and had tested the finer gauge on a machine that showed no appreciable reduction in drag from the thinner needle. But we didn't test it with the consumers, who have to stick these needles in themselves five or six times a day. They could feel the difference without even asking our machine, so they switched brands. Our problem was that even though we understood our competitors very well, we didn't have a good enough understanding of the market's unfulfilled needs. The planning session had given us a clear picture of the industry and the market, but only a static one. We weren't looking ahead.[3]

Consistency:
Does the Strategy Hang Together?

An effective strategy option is internally consistent, in the sense that each element of the strategy is part of an integrated pattern.

---

3. Becton-Dickinson case (D) (1982).

We need to be concerned about two levels of consistency. The first level is the fit of specific functional strategies with the basis for competitive advantage and the investment strategy that make up the strategic thrust. The second level of fit is concerned with the couplings among the functional strategies. Without an "acceptable" degree of fit at either level, effective coordination cannot be achieved. The obvious price is management energy needlessly devoted to organizational conflict and functional "finger pointing" to shift blame. A less obvious price is the consequence of the diffused and uncertain impression of the business in the market.

First-Level Consistency. The first question is whether the specific functional strategies of price, product design, service, technology, and so forth are compatible with the investment strategy. Are we emphasizing the right actions in support of a building, holding, or harvesting thrust? Useful insights can be gained by specifying the generic management strategies implied by the functional strategies,

Table 7.2 Matching Strategy Elements

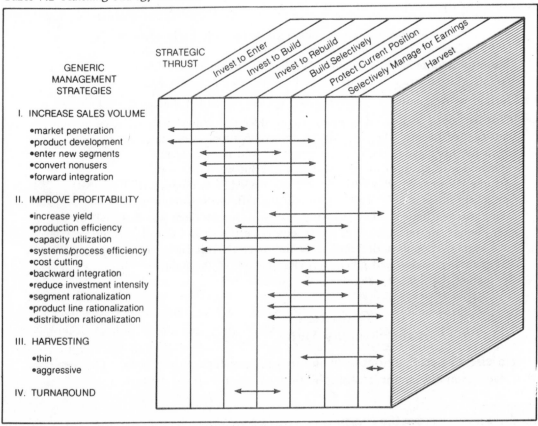

and then consulting Table 7.2 to see whether a consistent strategic thrust is evident. This table is built on the premise that certain logical combinations of generic management strategies, suitable for building and rebuilding, would be inappropriate if the emphasis were on selectively managing for earnings. As the emphasis shifts from a building to a holding position, the management strategies should then give greater emphasis to improving profitability.

The next concern at this level of consistency is whether the functional strategies also enhance the basis for competitive advantage. That is, when implemented, will they yield superiority in the skills and resources needed to support the desired basis for differentiation or achieve a low-cost position in the served market? Here, it is useful to go back to the analysis in Chapter 2 on the basis of a sustainable competitive advantage. The importance of this kind of consistency is highlighted by the strategy of the Provincetown-Boston Airline (PBA), which is arguably the most consistently profitable commuter airline carrier in the United States.

Throwing Conventional Wisdom to the Winds

PBA violates many of the established rules for airline success:

- PBA flies a largely resort trade. In the summer it serves the Cape Cod resort areas, and in the winter shifts focus to the Florida Gulf Coast. While they don't abandon routes during off-season, they relocate 50% of their aircraft (amounting to 70% of capacity) north in summer and south in winter.

- Conventional wisdom stresses the value of a limited number of modern, fuel-efficient types of aircraft for ease of operation and low maintenance costs. Instead PBA has five types of old aircraft, all of which have seen long service with many previous owners. The backbone of the fleet is 12 Douglas DC–3s which carry 30 passengers, but there are also 27 nine-passenger Cessna's and four 58-passenger Nihon YS–11s.

These resources and strategies give PBA its primary competitive advantage: the ability to balance capacity and demand. While PBA can cut costs during light traffic periods by flying smaller planes, they can afford to keep fully depreciated older aircraft on hand to fly additional sections of each flight. This means there is no overbooking, but load factors stay high. The result is low costs and consistent profitability.

Source: Hartman (1983).

Second-Level (Internal) Consistency.   A coordinated coupling of functional actions is difficult to achieve even when the basic strategy is unchanged; it is doubly difficult when considering a new strategy.[4] A capital goods manufacturer had for some years followed a strategy of producing to requisition. Each product was individually handled, and no finished inventory was carried. Consequently, many months could elapse between date of order and date of delivery. The thrust of a new aggressive share-building strategy was to gain a competitive advantage through product availability rather than through technology and performance characteristics. A key element of this strategy called for releasing certain models to manufacturing before firm orders were in hand, to shorten the delivery cycle.

Serious problems were encountered in implementation of this strategy. Customer complaints made it clear that the publicized reduction in delivery cycle had not been met. These complaints were expensive, for penalties were often imposed for late delivery. Additional unforeseen expenses came from the need to rework the models built for inventory to match them to the orders actually received. These problems were eventually traced to the incentives used in district sales offices. These incentives were based solely on the dollar size of orders, which was entirely congruent with the previous strategy of tailoring the product to met the special requirements of each customer. The measurement or incentive system contained no recognition that the new strategy required a different response to sell standardized products effectively. That the same sales force could sell both standardized and custom products was far from obvious.

The consistency test is seldom pivotal in that few strategies are rejected outright for inconsistency. More often, the test is used to improve and refine the strategy to ensure that all elements of the strategy are pointing in the same direction. One may conclude, however, that the degree of change necessary to bring the elements into line is simply not feasible with the available resources. Functional managers can cope with only a few changes while simultaneously trying to maintain continuing operations. Thus, upgrading old product lines, entering new markets, modernizing the costing system, and building a new manufacturing plant all at once may not be possible. For this reason, the next test of feasibility is often pivotal.

---

4. Hobbs and Heaney (1977).

Feasibility:
Do We Have the Skills, Resources,
and Commitment?

The feasibility test poses two questions of each strategy option:

1. Does the business possess the necessary skills and resources? If not, is there enough time to acquire or develop them before the strategic window closes?

2. Do the key operating personnel understand the underlying premises and elements of the option, and are they likely to be committed to implementing the option?

Assessing Skill and Resource Constraints.   Financial (capital funds or cash flow requirements) and physical resources are the first constraints against which the strategy option is tested. If these limitations are seriously constraining, to the point that competitive position is jeopardized, then the strategy has to be modified so the business can overcome or live within the constraint. One modification is innovative financing methods such as sale-leaseback arrangements or tying plant mortgages to long-term contracts. Another is to find a partner or sell out to a well-financed partner. The latter approach gave G.H. Bass and Company, the maker of the casual Bass Weejuns shoe brand, the resources to consolidate a strong market position.[5] In 1978, the collegiate look of their brand was becoming popular with other age groups and was able to command a price premium because of a quality image. Although the company was profitable, it was unable to take on any new customers because it lacked existing capacity and capital for expansion. By selling out to Chesebrough-Pond's, Inc. that year, it was able to tap the resources needed to fund a tripling of sales in three years. In that period, the company built a new distribution center, acquired two new shoe factories, and installed modern, computerized ordering and inventory control systems.

The next constraints to be tested are access to markets, technology, and servicing capabilities. Do we have adequate sales force coverage? Is the sales force adaptable to the selling job demanded by the strategic option? Is the advertising effort and effectiveness likely to be sufficient? What about the cost, efficiency, and coverage of the present distribution system—including order handling, warehousing, and delivery? Are relationships with jobbers, distrib-

---

5. *Business Week* (10 November 1980).

utors or retailers (or both), and service providers sufficiently secure to adapt to the proposed new strategy? Similarly, do we have sufficient knowledge and experience with the next generation of appropriate product and process technology? Negative or uncertain answers trigger a search for modifications to overcome problems, or perhaps will lead to eventual rejection of the option.

The most rigid constraints stem from the less quantifiable limitations of individuals and organizations. The basic question is whether the organization has ever shown it could muster the degree of coordinative and integrative skills necessary to carry out the change in strategy. Indeed, Rumelt [6] has argued that any strategy option in which success depends on accomplishing tasks that are outside the realm of reasonably attainable skills is unacceptable.

Capacity for Commitment.   A broad-based commitment to successful implementation comes when:

- the premises and elements of the strategy are readily communicable. If they are misinterpreted or not understood, then not only is the strategy option likely flawed, but also its capacity to motivate support is seriously compromised.

- the strategy option challenges and motivates key personnel. The option must not only have a champion who gives it enthusiastic and credible support, but also all key operating personnel must accept it. If these people have reservations, are not excited by its objectives and methods, or strongly support another option, the strategy must be judged infeasible.

Organizational commitment is essential—and the reasons lie at the very root of the nature of strategy [7] as a guiding force for the business:

> A strategy, as such, does not and cannot specify in detail each action that must be carried out. Its purpose is to provide structure to the general issue of the business goals and approaches to coping with its environment. It is up to the members and departments of the organization to carry out the tasks defined by the strategy.

---

6. Rumelt (1980).
7. Rumelt (1980).

Vulnerability:
What Are the Risks and Contingencies?

Each strategy option, and the associated projects, has a distinct risk profile. The overall level of risk reflects the vulnerability of key results if important assumptions are wrong or critical tasks are not accomplished. For example, an aggressive build strategy that increases investment intensity increases the break-even point. This makes that option more vulnerable to shortfalls in sales forecasts than a "manage for current earnings" option. In an unfamiliar market, this result is a distinct possibility; hence, this option is inherently risky.

The specific risk factors that contribute to the overall risk level can be either environmental or internal. The *environmental* risks should reflect the major uncertainties about the economic environment, competitor and market response, legislative and regulatory action, and the pace of technological change. These risks encompass such possibilities as price cutting by competitors, forward integration by suppliers, or weak market demand due to a recession. *Internal* risks are uncertainties about the ability of the business to execute a critical element of the strategy and thereby jeopardize performance. A delay in design or manufacturing could be critical if it meant the business missed a market development opportunity.

The Vulnerability/Opportunity Grid. As virtually any trend and internal capability is a potential risk factor, it is essential to isolate those few that would cause the most damage and deal with them explicitly. The vulnerability grid shown in Figure 7.1 is useful for this purpose. The *strategic importance* of the risk factors is a combination of (1) a sensitivity analysis of the potential consequences of extreme but plausible values—either positive or negative—of each factor on overall performance and (2) the likelihood that these extreme values could occur during the planning period. The appropriate response to important risk factors will depend on an assessment of the *degree of control* the business has over the factor. For example, those that are strategically important and are also subject to company control need to be understood very well, made the focus of major strategic action steps, and controlled tightly.

The specific risk factors illustrated in Figure 7.1 come from an assessment by a mining company of a major development proposal. The risky nature of the proposal is highlighted by the large number of strategically important risk factors such as mineral prices that are not controlled by the business. These become the focus of contingency plans and must continuously be monitored. For risk factors

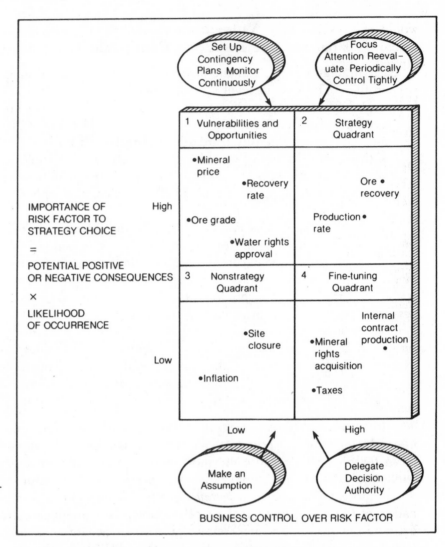

Figure 7.1 Vulnerability/Opportunity Grid for a Mining Company

that are strategically unimportant, it is sufficient to simply make an assumption or delegate authority to deal with the issue.

Adaptability: Can We Retain Our Flexibility?   In an uncertain environment, it is important to ask whether, and at what cost, the strategy could be reversed in the future. The purpose of this criterion is to extend the general criterion of vulnerability in search of ways to improve the strategy. This is not an argument against long-term investment in fixed plant and equipment, but in favor of finding the best ways to use the fixed commitments so that in the event of a major contingency occurring, a write off of the entire investment would not be necessary. What is the possibility for flexibility in design, multiple uses, or risk hedging—perhaps at a higher initial capital cost?

To be avoided is the situation that Monsanto encountered some years ago when it built a dedicated plant under contract to Coca-Cola. The product was an acrylonitrile plastic bottle to replace large glass bottles. Just when production had started, the FDA reversed its previous tentative approval of the new container. Despite court appeals, it was eventually necessary to abandon the acrylonitrile bottle and write off the investment in plant and equipment. The project had been vulnerable to this threat from the outset; the question is whether a different production concept, such as a plant that was designed to be convertible to other materials, was feasible. If so, such a move would have reduced the company's exposure to this risk.

The criterion of adaptability applies equally to decisions to delay changes in strategic direction or to undertake major investment programs. The implications of delay are difficult to assess, especially when they are buried in the implicit assumption of discounted cash flow analysis that investments are reversible. Specifically, it is assumed that if one delays an investment, one can always make it at some later date with no penalty other than that implied by the company's discount rate. To regain this lost ground, the business may have to spend a good deal more than if it had made the investment when first proposed. If the strategic window has closed, no opportunity may be available to adapt to the new situation, and all flexibility would be lost.

Potential Rewards:
What Are the Forecast Outcomes?

The ultimate test of the final candidate options is the forecast of their respective outcomes. Three classes of measures can be used for this purpose:

1. Economic value generation
2. Sales growth and profitability
3. Relative competitive position

The sales growth and profitability measures—including ROS, net earnings, ROI, RONA, and cash flow—are the most widely used benchmarks for evaluating strategy options. As they are readily available from the financial accounting system, they are also influential measures of performance. Unfortunately, they are seldom adequate for sending meaningful signals to corporate- or business-level decision makers. There are increasingly persuasive arguments that superior signals come from evaluating the merits of a strategy option in light of its capacity to enhance the economic value of the business or to improve competitive position.

Economic Value Measures.   Earnings and related accounting measures of profitability such as RONA and ROI have several shortcomings as financial standards by which strategic options can be compared:

- earnings figures do not consider possible differences in the risk exposure of strategic options
- estimates of accounting earnings are susceptible to distortion from differences arising from the way cost of sales and depreciation are determined
- there is no consideration of the time value of the earnings stream, i.e., what is the value of a dollar of earnings received two years hence versus next year?

A measure that overcomes these problems is obtained by discounting the anticipated cash flows from the strategy option by the risk-adjusted cost of capital for the business unit.[8] This discount rate is obtained by multiplying the corporate cost of capital (both debt and equity) by an index that reflects the inherent riskiness of the business and the strategy option. Higher risk indexes are assigned when (1) the past performance of the business has been characterized by high year-to-year variance in profits or large variances between planned and actual forecast (or both) and (2) the strategy option is inherently risky. Indicators of the risk of the option are the rate of growth of the business relative to competition, the familiarity of the business with the product-markets being entered, and the specific risk factors identified in the vulnerability/opportunity grid.

For a strategy option to create economic value, the discounted cash flow must be positive and exceed the cost of financing that option. This is a minimum condition that any option must satisfy if it is to be worthy of further consideration. However, it doesn't necessarily tell us whether the option is the best one for the busi-

---

8. Rappaport (1981).

ness or as attractive for corporate investment as options in other businesses. To answer these questions it is necessary to compute an overall value/book ratio, to take account of differing levels of investment between the options being compared. For this analysis overall value is estimated by adding the discounted terminal value of the business (assuming, for example, the business was sold after 10 years), to the discounted cash flows from the option. This is divided by the book value of the business, obtained from the balance sheet. The higher the value/book ratio the more attractive the option.

Competitive Position Measures.   The forecast of substantial creation of economic value—or of high rates of profitability—cannot be taken as automatic indicators of the acceptability of a strategic option. Both these measures must be based on persuasive evidence of anticipated scarcity or competitive advantage.[9] Thus, further tests of the outcomes require forecasts of the likelihood the option will gain or sustain a positional advantage. For this purpose what is needed is persuasive evidence that anticipated levels or changes in the following measures can be achieved:

1. Market shares
   - served market
   - market segments
2. Relative cost position
3. Relative quality level
4. Share of industry production capacity
5. Share of advertising expenditures and distribution coverage
6. Sales force coverage
7. Awareness and attitude

The advantages of these measures are that they are closer to the basis of competitive advantage and thus can be used to monitor the accomplishment of the strategy when it is implemented.

The Hierarchy of Outcomes.   No single measure or class of measures is adequate for evaluating or comparing strategy options. Each class of measures sheds light on a different facet of the forecast performance. It does not follow, however, that they can be treated as

---

9. Wensley (1981).

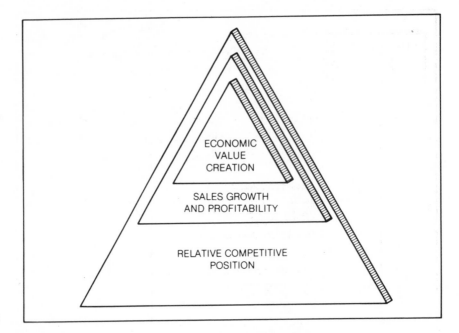

Figure 7.2
Hierarchy of
Strategy Outcomes

independent, for the relationships among them are very close as shown in Figure 7.2. Thus, poor performance on any one measure is grounds for raising questions about the overall desirability of the option.

Applying the Evaluation Criteria: Selecting the Strategic Option

The evaluation stage is a learning process, as strategies are successively tested, refined, and retested against the criteria. This process is illustrated in Figure 7.3. Some of the criteria are sufficiently robust that the option can be eliminated from consideration. Seldom, however, does a clearly dominant strategic option emerge from this analysis. Instead, a choice has to be made by balancing rewards against the risks and the magnitude of the investment commitment. This judgment is negotiated between business unit and corporate management, in light of the attractiveness of other investment opportunities and the degree to which the provisional objectives are satisfied by any of the options.

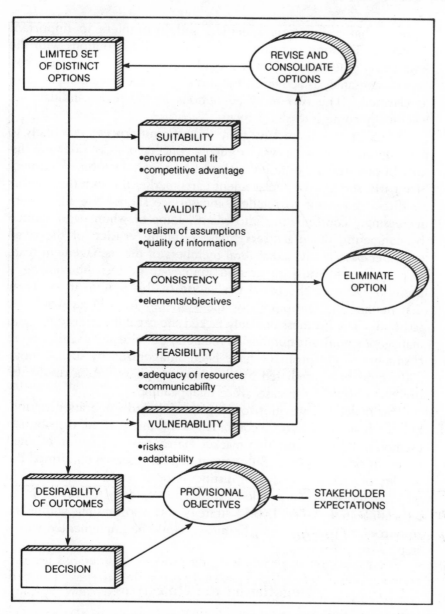

Figure 7.3 Evaluating Strategic Options

Refining and Combining Options

The process of refining strategies is like refining a metal from an ore body loaded with impurities. The purpose is to separate the best features of each strategy option from the residue of infeasible and unsuitable elements. The departure point is a set of strategy options that are loosely specified and incomplete in important respects. Through successive screenings of these options with the evaluation criteria, which also provide direction to information collection and analysis activities, the thinking of the management team is clarified. The two or three options in the final candidate set eventually come into sharp focus.

When an option emerges from the refining process, it is likely to be different from what was originally conceived. Consider the history of one strategy option developed by a manufacturer of automotive parts, serving the replacement parts market through distributors or direct shipments to retailers and service shops. Retailers were increasingly consolidating into chains, some of whom were owned by competing manufacturers. The resulting erosion of the retail customer base motivated several members of the management team to propose a forward integration strategy to protect the company's position. During the initial evaluation of this option, it was clear that neither the feasibility nor the vulnerability criteria would be satisfied. The business not only lacked the capability to acquire and manage a significant number of retailers, but also the existing retail customers would probably have been antagonized by such a move and would have retaliated by switching suppliers. As a result, the preliminary profit forecasts were unappealing.

The resolution was not to drop the forward integration option, but to develop a hybrid combination of the current distribution method in regions with high market shares, plus acquisition of retail chains in other regions. Subsequent market research confirmed the validity of such a strategy, for distinct regions could be identified in which a move would not jeopardize the company's position in an adjacent region. This hybrid strategy was also feasible within the resources and was less risky because it could be implemented with a step-by-step program.

Negotiating the Objectives

Early in the planning process, the magnitude of the required change in strategy was defined by the gap between what the business could likely achieve by continuing the present strategy and the preliminary expectations of corporate management for revenue, earnings growth, and profitability.

We are now at the point where the potential "gap-filling" strategies have been identified along with their probable outcomes. The first indication of the need for negotiation of objectives comes from the assessment of the economic value contribution of the feasible options. The options for each business must not only be compared, but also corporate management must consider the options from other businesses in light of this criterion. Conceivably, none of the options will be satisfactory, and further modifications will be required to improve cash flows or to reduce the risk exposure.

The next step is to translate the chosen strategy into specific objectives that can serve to guide the actions of operating management and to monitor subsequent performance. For these purposes, the measures of strategic outcomes based on sales growth and profitability, and of relative competitive position, are more useful. Corporate management will generally cast their initial expectations for the business in these terms as well. Further negotiation is necessary if the objectives do not satisfy these expectations—negotiation either to adjust the objectives or to scale down the expectations. This approach often requires shifting the priority assigned to one class of objectives, such as profitability, to another class, such as market position.

Objectives are ultimately chosen within the constraints of what is strategically feasible. As one planner notes, "Objectives must be challenging but achievable. Otherwise, the whole process of planning is compromised and may turn into an expensive exercise in futility and frustration."

Pitfalls and Biases in Strategy Selection

The final choice of strategy option and associated program elements will reflect the outcome of strenuous negotiations and complex judgments about risk, reward, and resource trade-offs in ambiguous environments. Not surprisingly, decision makers strive to simplify these decisions and hence to reduce their uncertainty and stress. In so doing, however, they may afflict their judgments with serious biases. The overt consequences are unrealistic forecasts and simplistic financial judgments.

Unrealistic Forecasts

The bane of managers and planners is the "hockey-stick" forecast, also known as the rolling-J-curve forecast. The comparison of three sets of long-range forecasts against actual performance in Figure 7.4 is a good example of this type of forecast. Despite the serious discrepancy between actual and forecast earnings in 1977 and 1978, the management of this business was still holding to unrealistic assumptions about share stability and strengthening mar-

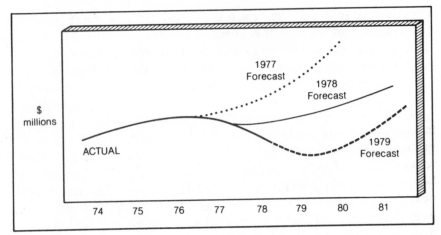

1977
Forecast

1978
Forecast

$
millions

ACTUAL

1979
Forecast

74   75   76   77   78   79   80   81

Figure 7.4 Earnings History and Forecast

gins. Their only concession to reality was an acknowledgment that the turnaround would be more difficult than first anticipated.

Four sources of bias that underlie this pattern of wishful thinking have been identified by decision theorists: [10]

1. *Availability.* This bias arises because evaluations of strategic options are likely to be dominated by facts and opinions that are easy to retrieve. Often, what is available is evidence of the past success of a strategy. Because hard data such as this are given more weight than qualitative assessments of future threats, management may be unrealistically complacent.

2. *Anchoring.* Decision makers also tend to "anchor" on a particular outcome value they believe will occur. This outcome dominates their thinking about the option and suppresses consideration of uncertainties. As a result, downside risks are understated.

3. *Selective perception.* Several biasing elements are present here: people tend to structure problems in light of their past experience (marketing people will interpret a general management problem as a marketing problem), the anticipation of what one expects to see will influence what one actually sees, and as a consequence, conflicting evidence will be disregarded.

---

10. See Tversky and Kahneman (1974) and Gardner and Thomas (1983). A comprehensive review has recently been provided by Hogarth and Makridakis (1981).

4. *Illusion of control.*   Planning activities may give decision makers the illusion that they can master and control their environment.   At the same time, decision makers have a tendency to attribute success to their own efforts and failure to external events.

These four problems are compounded when top management has unrealistic expectations and requires operating management to make commitments that may not be possible.   Texas Instruments is reputedly [11] a company in which senior management created a number of long-term problems by forcing operating managers to accept nearly impossible goals.   Meetings to review operations and plans were designed to generate a "We'll make it happen" attitude rather than figure out where TI was going.   The result was that after senior management got the commitment they wanted, operating management then had to decide how to make it happen.   In the view of one consultant who worked with TI, "The planning sessions generate false hope, not business plans."

As in all facets of planning, the key is hard-nosed reality and a willingness to support challenging objectives with adequate resources.   This approach has worked well for TI in some areas, such as its terrain-following radar system for the F–18 jet fighter and its seismographic system for oil exploration that shows underground formations in three dimensions.   The pressure of unrealistic objectives, however, can also force operating management to attempt programs that are beyond their capabilities, as when TI lost ground in the home computer market by trying to write most of its own software.

Inappropriate Financial Assessments

The myopia and biases that afflict managers' judgments have especially serious consequences for financial evaluations of investments in strategies and projects.[12]   For example, while much effort is devoted to projecting market growth, simplifying assumptions are often made that prices will move and shares will behave as they have in the past.   Price levels, however, may be depressed either by too much added capacity or by low-cost capacity additions that displace high-cost facilities.   The problem is even encountered in

---

11. Uttal (1982).
12. Rudden (1982).

straightforward discounted cash flow analyses of the gains from cost-reducing investments. Yet, other companies are making similar investments. Thus, if prices reflect the changing cost structure of a competitive industry, the actual earnings may be lower than expected. This possibility may help explain why most companies' returns fall far short of their hurdle rates for investment.

Overcoming the Biases

Two complementary approaches should be considered. The first is to shift the analysis of strategic options away from vulnerable measures such as discounted cash flows or internal rates of return, and instead focus on fundamental determinants of the profit potential of the business, such as competitive quality and cost position. At the same time, the planning system should encourage constructive debate and criticism about these fundamental factors and should reduce possible resistance to challenges of the conventional wisdom. These outcomes can be facilitated by using recently developed methods for testing strategic assumptions, which are described in the Appendix to this chapter.

Summary

The essence of a business strategy is an integrated set of actions in the pursuit of a competitive advantage. In this chapter, we amplified our understanding of strategy by establishing the criteria for an effective strategy. While these criteria were developed for the immediate purpose of guiding the choice from among a set of strategic options, they are equally appropriate for assessing the adequacy of the present business strategy. Their value lies in guiding our thinking and evaluation in productive directions.

An Effective Business Strategy

The message of the evaluation criteria is that an effective strategy:

- exploits environmental trends and creates a sustainable competitive advantage
- is based on realistic assumptions and accurate information
- can be achieved with the available resources
- is internally consistent

- is acceptable to the operating managers who will be responsible for implementation
- is flexible enough to respond to unexpected developments
- will achieve the performance objectives of the stakeholders without requiring undue risks

Appendix   Testing Strategic Assumptions

This section describes a process that has been developed specifically to surface underlying assumptions, critically examine them, and then make informed judgments. The distinguishing features of SAST (Strategic Assumptions Surfacing and Testing) [13] are:

- The starting point is the basic set of strategy options that management is considering. Instead of the normal planning process, in which assumptions are specified during the situation assessment and strategy options are developed, the sequence is reversed, and the outcome is the evaluation of a set of assumptions.

- The procedure is *adversarial* in that it relies on controlled conflict between groups. Formally, it is based on the notion of dialectical inquiry, in which every course of action or thesis has an alternative incompatible course of action or an antithesis. The decision reflects a synthesis of the conflicting viewpoints.

- The procedure is *participative,* because the involvement of users and providers of information is necessary to achieve a full understanding of complex issues.

- It is *integrative,* because merely criticizing a proposed strategy is not sufficient. Strong points from various perspectives need to be combined to form a strategy that has support of key individuals and organizations.

A representative application of SAST was recently described by Barabba.[14] This application is actually a composite of several similar strategic choices that Kodak faced. The specific issue was whether Kodak should continue to manufacture and sell amateur movie cameras. Available were three distinct strategy options, each with strong advocates:

A1:   Continue to manufacture and sell movie cameras to take advantage of a strong European market.

A2:   Exit the movie camera market, but continue to sell movie film to current users as well as to any new customers.

---

13. Emshoff and Finnel (1979) and Mason, Mitroff, and Barabba (1980).
14. Barabba (1981).

A3: Sustain current position in the United States and manufacture low-cost products designed for developing
countries.

The SAST process for dealing with this kind of messy choice situation, in which no alternative is dominant, has five stages: (1) group
formation, (2) assumptions surfacing and rating, (3) debate among
groups, (4) information requirements analysis, and (5) synthesis and
decision. The process can also be adapted fairly readily to situations in which the options or answers have not been defined in
advance.

Group Formation

For each strategic option, a group of advocates is formed. Each
group should be as internally homogenous as possible and as different from every other group as possible. All the groups, collective-
ly, must represent broad coverage of the different functional
perspectives on the strategic decision. Putting like-minded individuals in the same group helps minimize conflict during the early
stages of the process and ensures the strongest possible arguments
in support of each option.

Assumptions Surfacing and Rating

The purpose of this step is to draw out all the assumptions that
logically form the underpinnings for a particular strategy option.
This surfacing is greatly facilitated by first identifying the people
that the choice will affect. These stakeholders include those who
have an interest in the strategy, are in a position to influence its
adoption or execution, or because of their characteristics ought to
care about the outcome.

When stakeholders have been identified, each advocacy group
asks, What must we assume about each stakeholder for our chosen
strategy option to be successful? To test the importance of each of
these assumptions, the group is then told to generate a counterassumption. If the counterassumption is true but would not have a
significant impact on the strategy, then it is likely that this assumption is not very relevant to the problem. Finally, each of the
remaining assumptions is rated in terms of relative *importance* and
relative *certainty,* and is plotted on a grid. An illustrative grid from
an analysis of the launch strategy for a new telecommunications

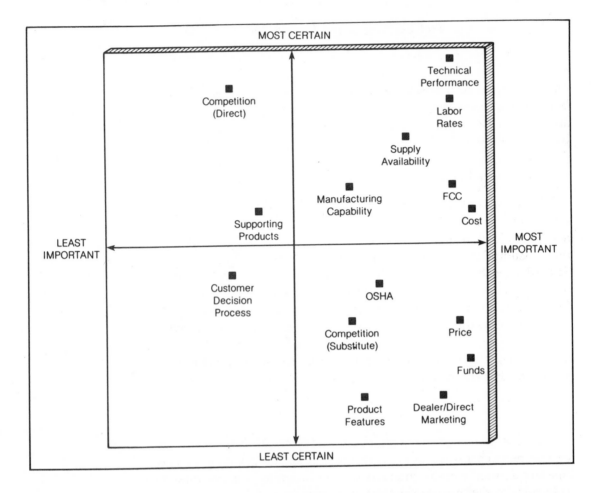

Figure 7.5 Assumption Plotting Grid

product is shown in Figure 7.5. The "most certain" assumptions are those the group believed were most likely to be true.

With the aid of the Assumption Plotting Grid, each group identifies the six to eight pivotal assumptions that should become the fundamental premises of their strategy option. For example, the Kodak group that wanted to exit the amateur movie camera market assumed that U.S. consumers no longer wanted to make home movies. In support of this premise, they cited declining sales in the United States, a dropping birth rate, an older population, and competition from videocassette recorders. By contrast, the group advocating a sustaining strategy assumed that people would buy a low-cost movie camera and that Kodak could make one. Their supporting arguments were that the technology was available, young people were more visually oriented, and many people believed the price of current home movie cameras was too high.

Debate Among Groups

At this point, the advocacy groups meet to present their positions and to challenge each other's assumptions. The emphasis is on identifying differences in stakeholders or in assumptions (or both) and encouraging debates that can surface additional considerations. The outcome is a list of *critical issues* on which no consensus has been reached.

Information Requirements Analysis

The remaining issues are important assumptions that carry high levels of uncertainty. These issues become the focal point for information collection activities. The Kodak groups were divided in their assumptions about consumer attitudes toward home movies. This division became the focal point of a series of research studies involving a reanalysis of historical data in the information system, focus group studies, and a segmentation analysis of the probable target markets. Critical issues can also be used to identify environmental trends that require continuous monitoring. One of the major benefits of the SAST process is that it focuses research efforts to ensure that the resulting information is strategically relevant.

Synthesis and Decision

The previous stages involve controlled conflict between advocacy groups. This stage requires a mood of collaboration to resolve the outstanding issues. The basis for resolution may be information collected for that purpose, a revision of assumptions by one or more groups, or perhaps a modification of the initial strategic options. The final decision is, however, made outside the SAST process. To the degree that it reflects assumptions on which there is significant consensus by all participants in the process, it is likely to be accepted and successfully implemented.

Field studies of the application of SAST—or dialectical inquiry systems in general—have reported satisfaction with the process [15] and better decisions. One study found that the process was successful in meeting three criteria: (1) the final strategy was acceptable to senior management, (2) the planning group did not become fractionated, and (3) the final strategy was forecast to be effective. These field studies have aroused a lively debate among supporters

---

15. Mason and Mitroff (1981).

of an alternative but simpler procedure using a *devil's advocate*.[16] This procedure involves assigning someone the explicit role of critiquing a proposed plan and bringing out all the reasons why the proposal should not be accepted. Both methods have the same intent, but differ in whether there is an explicit search for an alternative strategy. Further research will no doubt find that each is appropriate in different circumstances reflecting different degrees of uncertainty. Regardless of the technique used, the value of any searching examination of the premises underlying a strategy is the minimization of uncertainty and the satisfaction of the criteria for an effective strategy.

16. Cosier and Aplin (1980).

Implementing Strategic Decisions

Chapter 8

The arduous process of analysis, adaptation, and negotiation that culminates in the choice of a strategic thrust and supporting strategies will come to naught unless equal care is given to translating the strategic decision into a course of action. The primary vehicles for managing this translation are:

Nothing chastens a planner more than the knowledge that he will have to carry out the plan.

—General Gavin

- specific action programs
- budgets and resource allocation procedures
- period plans for the business unit and functional activities, and
- control processes

These implementation vehicles are normally tied together within a formal planning system that establishes the procedures and the time sequence of planning events. Our primary purpose in this chapter is to discuss these aspects of implementation and the pitfalls that must be avoided if they are to be effective. The broad question of implementation has many other aspects that are beyond the scope of this chapter, including the design of the organization, the selection of managers and their incentives, and the organizational climate. These elements must support and enhance the direct mechanisms that are our concern in this chapter. As in all matters of strategy, congruency of effort is critical to success.

The greater the departure from the current strategy, the greater the need for effective implementation planning. The established policies, structures, and resource commitments have all been put in place expressly to carry out the old strategy. No matter how well the new strategy addresses the issues and opportunities of the future, the likelihood of success is small unless there is a conscious and appropriate break in these established patterns. This was the bitter lesson that Standard Brands learned in the late seventies as a new management team attempted to overcome the legacy of a short-run financial orientation that resulted in long-term weakening of such brands as Chase and Sanborn coffee, Curtiss candy, Planters nuts and Fleischmann liquor. Because of a history of poor new product development performance, the company had become overly dependent on the cyclical corn syrup refining business. The new team's efforts to diversify and reduce this dependence produced some of the most celebrated failures in the food industry.[1] Among the problems were an inability to produce acceptable additions to the product lines of acquisitions such as Pinata Foods, or to mount marketing campaigns that were effective against entrenched competitors such as Frito-Lay. Further, time was not taken to streamline the antiquated sales force. As a result, Standard Brands continued to send separate sales forces to make duplicate calls on supermarket chains. The lesson the company learned from this experience was that good strategies cannot effectively be implemented from the headquarters. The programs must have the involvement and commitment of the line operating managers. Many companies have also learned that strategy by itself is not enough. Attention to the details of implementation is just as important.

Translating Strategic Decisions into Actions

Within a business unit, action steps are spelled out in programs, short-range functional plans, and budgets. Each of these elements fits logically within the umbrella framework of strategic direction and supporting management strategies spelled out in the strategic plan. The relationship of these implementation activities to the overall strategy formulation process is shown below in Figure 8.1. The functional plans and action programs are both an output of this process and the basis for the specific performance criteria and measures to be used to monitor and control strategic performance. The comparison of actual against desired performance is a major input to a situation assessment, and so the planning process is renewed.

Programs embrace specific tasks, such as developing a new product, improving the productivity of an operating unit, or launching a

---

1. *Business Week* (18 February 1980).

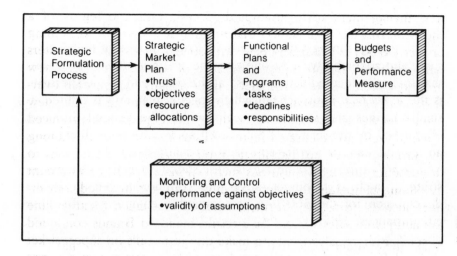

Figure 8.1 Implementation Planning

new advertising campaign. A program usually focuses on a single objective, but may involve several functions within the organization. The time horizon is determined by the urgency of the task, the designated resources, and the need to coordinate with related programs.

Functional plans are necessary for integration of the various programs for change in direction, as well as to ensure the organization effectively manages the continuing operations of the business. The choice of the functions for which detailed plans are prepared and linked to the strategic business plan will depend on the focus of the strategy. Most organizations have annual marketing plans and production plans, but not necessarily a distinct plan for computer systems unless such systems are integral to performance. The time horizon of such plans is usually short—a matter of one to two years at the most. The cycle for review and decision making, however, is closely tied to the calendar to ensure an operating budget exists for each function at the beginning of the fiscal year.

Budgets are the most detailed and sometimes the most time-consuming manifestation of the planning process. The essence of budgeting is to attach a dollar figure to each income- and expense-related activity. The use of a common denominator for activities permits the integration of all aspects of the strategy within the available resources. Because budgets reflect the allocation of these resources, they become essential guides to action. They also set standards for coordinating activities and eventually become one of the benchmarks against which performance can be assessed.

Approaches to Program Development

Program planning varies greatly in scope, degree of detail, time span, and adaptability.[2] At one extreme are *comprehensive* programs that spell out detailed action steps; at the other end of the spectrum is the *incremental* approach, in which specific planning is limited to small changes and short time spans within the general direction established by the strategy. Since each approach has its limitations, an intermediate or *selective* approach is usually desirable.

Comprehensive programming is best suited to major changes in strategy, such as Boeing's move into commercial jets or IBM's development of the 360 line of compatible computers. In these circumstances,

1. the strategic objective is clear-cut, and management has made a strong commitment,
2. it is important to meet a difficult schedule, either to pre-empt competitors or to get through a "strategic window,"
3. the resources are available and not too deeply immersed in existing operations, and
4. success depends on the coordination of many disparate functions.

The *incremental* approach is best suited to situations in which uncertainty is considerable such as when developing a new geographic market or launching an R and D program. Initial estimates of outcomes, timing, costs, and resource requirements are based on assumptions that are likely to change. The argument for postponing and restricting detailed programming is that long-term programs will have to be revised to adapt to the inevitable change, so why reduce flexibility unnecessarily? Instead, the next years' programs are built on the outcomes of current programs and the prevailing conditions within the broad framework of the business objectives and strategy. Important elements of the strategy are sometimes left deliberately vague to reflect major contingencies. For example, some new entrants into the personal computer market have detailed programs for designing and sourcing the hardware and software, but have postponed specific plans for distribution until the options are more fully explored. This gives them some flexibility to exploit changes in channel options without being constrained by prior decisions.

---

2. Yavitz and Newman (1982).

Selective Programming.   The conditions for successful comprehensive programming are seldom encountered in the execution of business strategies.   Incrementalism, however, may also be inappropriate. If programs are designed only to deal with the next steps, the impetus necessary to mount a big change may never be developed. The preferred approach is to concentrate on developing detailed programs in selective areas where:

a. a high payoff is likely (such as assuring the basis for competitive advantage is developed and nurtured),
b. the action is a necessary first step in a sequence, as is usually the case in building a new manufacturing capability because of the long lead times, or
c. protecting a future resource allocation is necessary.

A business unit contemplating a new strategic direction that utilizes a shared corporate resource, such as a central R and D facility or a pooled sales force, may have to build a persuasive action program to make the case that the resource should be developed or reserved even though it is not yet needed.

The outcome of selective programming is a clear set of action priorities and short-term resource requirements and organizational responsibilities within the broad framework of the business strategy.

The Structure and Content of Plans

Eisenhower observed wisely that "Plans are nothing; planning is everything." Nonetheless, large, integrated, multifunctional businesses need written documentation of their strategic decisions, both to *communicate* the logic and assumptions of the strategy to all managers who will be asked to implement the plan, and to provide a basis for budgeting and *resource allocation* decisions. Other important purposes are to identify the specific action steps and timetables that have been assigned to individual managers or teams, and to provide a performance standard against which actual progress can be compared.

The types of plans used by a company to achieve these purposes depend on the type of industry, the role of marketing within the organization, and the stage of evolution of their planning practices. Among firms that have adopted strategic planning or strategic management, an integrated strategic market or business plan is usually prepared for each business, with a variety of possible supporting plans for major programs and functions. Indeed, each business oft-

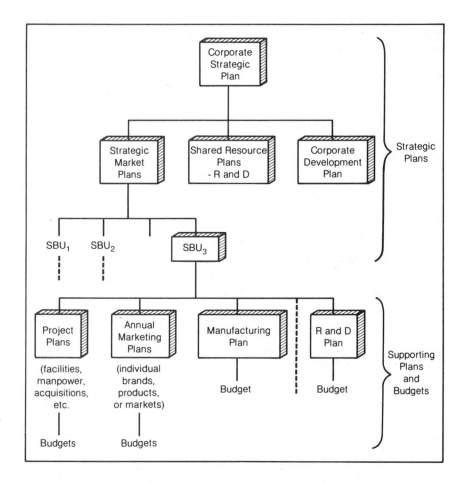

Figure 8.2 Hierarchy of Strategic Plans

en has a whole family of plans and budgets, arranged in a hierarchy as shown in Figure 8.2.

The content of the market plan should incorporate all the important judgments, assumptions, contingencies, and choices made during the planning process. Useful plans are difficult to prepare, for they must be concise and yet communicate effectively to the management team. If the document fails on either of these dimensions, it will not serve as a useful, living guide to ongoing strategic decisions. At worst, it may simply be filed away and surface again only when the next planning exercise is begun. Table 8.1 outlines a format that has been successfully used by a number of businesses to create usable, living documents that effectively summarize management thinking.

Table 8.1 Format for a Strategic Market Plan

A. PLANNING SITUATION
- business definition
- performance versus prior plan objectives
- corporate guidelines

B. PLAN OVERVIEW
- one-page summary of situation, strategy, and forecast results

C. SITUATION ASSESSMENT
1. Market analysis and segmentation
2. Competitor analysis
3. Major trends in environment
4. Internal capabilities and current position in served markets
5. Cost and profit analysis

D. SITUATION SUMMARY
1. Planning assumptions
2. Market attractiveness and business strength analysis
3. Strategic issues

E. STRATEGIC DECISIONS AND ACTION PROGRAMS
1. Business strategy
   - objectives
   - thrust
   - supporting functional strategies
2. Key programs
   - strategy elements
   - resource requirements
   - timing and responsibilities
3. Discarded options

F. FINANCIAL SUMMARY
- performance
- risks
- validity test

G. CONTINGENCIES

Supporting Functional Plans.   It is increasingly common to find that functional plans are being integrated into a business or strategic market plan.   Nowhere is this integration more evident than with the marketing plan.   A recent study [3] found that this had occurred in more than 40 percent of a large sample of companies.   The results of this study are presented in Table 8.2.

If a marketing or sales plan is prepared in conjunction with a strategic market plan, it usually serves to elaborate the short-term (one-year) tactical programs such as media scheduling and sales force allocation.   Consumer product firms are likely to have such plans for major brands or product lines.   Such plans are also useful within firms in which corporate marketing support is extensive, perhaps because of a pooled sales force or distribution system, or because of the need to integrate advertising and sales promotion activities.

Table 8.2 The Role of the Marketing Plan

	TYPE OF FIRM		
	Industrial Products ($n = 134$)	Consumer Products ($n = 97$)	Services ($n = 30$)
A separate marketing plan is prepared for each major product	34%	46%	17%
A single integrated marketing plan covers all major products	20	20	40
A marketing plan is not a separate document, but instead forms part of a broader strategic plan	46	34	43
	100%	100%	100%

3. Hopkins (1981).

Strategic Planning Systems

Strategic planning should not be an isolated event that culminates in a clear-cut decision. Instead, it should be an ongoing activity that responds simultaneously to the pressures of events and the dictates of the calendar. To ensure organizational commitment, involvement must come from many levels of the organization, for each has a distinct role in formulating the strategy and ensuring the integration of corporate resource allocations, strategies and objectives, and action plans. The purpose of the planning system is to integrate these activities and specify when each step is to be completed.

The Multicycle Planning System

Strategic planning follows three basic approaches, differing primarily in the locus of important inputs, analyses, and decisions. The first is the *top-down* approach, in which the strategic planning is done primarily at the top of the organization. Guidelines are given to the business units, who then prepare short-range plans within these guidelines. The plans are reviewed by corporate management and either accepted or sent back for modifications. The obvious disadvantages are that corporate management lacks the detailed information necessary to formulate the guidelines, and the operating managers may feel constrained by such centralized direction.

With the *bottom-up* approach, the business units are given no explicit guidelines other than to formulate and submit plans according to a designated format and schedule. The resulting strategy recommendations, with resource requirements and forecast performance results, are then reviewed by senior management. This approach has some serious problems in practice: [4]

> Typically, these review sessions are long and gruelling affairs, demoralizing for down-the-line managers and frustrating at best for their superiors. In today's complex business environment, few senior executives can know enough about their companies' various businesses to make any positive contribution to the proposals presented to them for decision; and at any rate, by the time they see a proposal it is usually too late to make real changes. As a result, top managers

---

4. Hunsicker (1980).

have the choice of approving a project about which they may have reservations, rejecting it altogether, or ordering a crash program to redo in days or weeks a proposal that may have taken months to put together in the first place.

Integrated Approaches.   Both top-down and bottom-up approaches are inherently unbalanced.   As a consequence, most decentralized companies have evolved systems in which continuing dialogue is present among all levels of management.   The basic elements of this approach are diagramed [5] in Figure 8.3.   As can be seen, each cycle in this system involves all levels of management, who must reach agreement on various aspects of the strategy before the next cycle begins.

Cycle I: Guidelines, Issues, and Options.   This cycle begins with corporate management providing broad guidelines to each business in the following areas:

a. Environmental assumptions. To ensure compatibility of plans and budgets, it is necessary that all business units make the same assumptions about inflation, economic growth, currency values, and the availability of capital.

b. Preliminary expectations about the performance of the business in key result areas such as profitability (short and long run), market position, ratio of cash usage to cash generated, and revenue growth. These expectations should be regarded as highly tentative and subject to further negotiation, for the appropriate objectives will also depend on the strategic position of the business and the willingness of corporate management to fund new initiatives.

c. Specific strategic issues to be considered during the planning process. Here, corporate management can express their concerns by highlighting specific developments they believe will adversely impact on the ability of the business to meet its objectives. In addition, they may nominate a few companywide priorities, such as quality, inventory control, or productivity, to which each business unit must respond with a focused action program. Finally, corporate management may identify opportunities for coordination

---

5. This representation of the planning process is adapted from a similar approach described by Lorange and Vancil (1977) and Abell and Hammond (1979).

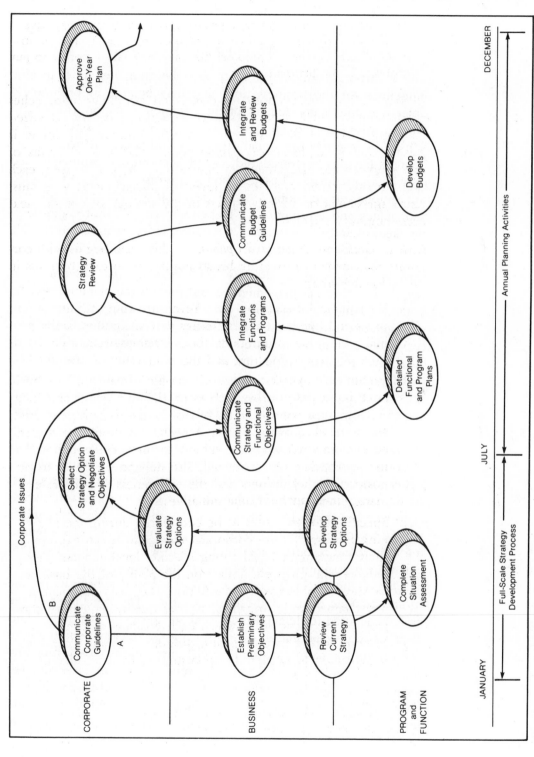

Figure 8.3 Multicycle Planning System

among several business units to ensure adequate coverage of an emerging market opportunity.

These corporate guidelines must then be translated into specific guidelines for the business unit, and may emerge as preliminary objectives and as an element of the complete situation assessment. During this cycle, the emphasis is on exploring the feasible options. While the specific functional strategies and their financial consequences have to be considered, the projections and estimates need only be approximate. Instead, the focus is on creativity in formulating options and on taking a broad view that will encompass all relevant issues and assumptions. Depending on the thoroughness of the analysis and the amount of new information required, this cycle may last six or more months.

Cycle II: Negotiation of Objectives and Strategies and Detailed Planning. Corporate management should reenter the planning process at the beginning of this cycle. Evidence is growing[6] that corporate management can make a far more effective contribution to the process when several options are still open, fewer positions have hardened, and relatively little time has been invested in the detailed development of a specific option. By contrast, attempts to make substantive inputs late in the process are difficult and may be perceived as counterproductive or threatening. The pivotal step is the "negotiation of objectives," in which corporate and operating management engage in an ongoing dialogue so each party understands the other's position. On one hand, corporate management gains a better appreciation of the opportunities and the need for resources. At the same time, operating management gets much clearer signals as to whether corporate management has adequate resources and is willing to commit them to aggressive new initiatives, or is attempting to husband resources and simply wants a fine tuning of the present strategy to improve short-run earnings performance.

Out of the Cycle II dialogue comes a broad consensus on the future strategic thrust of the business unit. The remainder of the cycle is devoted to detailed functional and program planning. This requires more elaboration of the specific product-market strategies and careful forecasting of the financial implications. Each functional program will be costed, and the total impact on expenses, net income, cash flow, and investment requirements will be considered. During the latter part of this cycle, the programs are integrated and tested for consistency. Particular attention has to be paid to con-

---

6. Hunsicker (1981) and Charan (1982).

flicts between programs and possible shared resource constraints. For example, a major insurance company, undertaking aggressive build strategies in two business segments—group life and health and group pensions—discovered that the sales force did not have the capacity or capability to obtain the desired volume increases and would have to be expanded significantly, while several systems bottlenecks would slow the pace of development. The resolution of these conflicting requirements required significant changes in the detailed strategies.

The output of this cycle is an integrated strategic market plan and complete functional plans for each major activity area such as manufacturing, sales, services, physical distribution, and research and development.

Cycle III: Strategy Review and Annual Planning. This cycle begins with a thorough corporate review of the validity and reality of the specific strategy, and a further test against the corporate goals, resource availability, and constraints. Here, corporate management seeks to understand the trade-offs that the business management was forced to make and the assumptions about key success factors. They will also be looking carefully for implications for other business units.

The depth of the review will vary with the amount of prior participation of corporate management in the shaping of the options in the earlier cycles of the planning process. From the strategy review comes a commitment by corporate management to the strategy and resource requirements, as modified during the review. Business management also commit themselves to delivering certain results. Subsequent operating reviews during the coming year provide for monitoring and follow-up of this commitment.

Most of the third cycle activity will be devoted to the preparation of the annual plan for the coming fiscal year. Specific forecasts for each revenue and cost element become extremely important at this stage, for their timing will have significant implications for budgets and resource requirements. From commitments and forecasts, the specific pro forma income statements, balance sheets, and cash flow statements can be prepared. These are the basis for the specific budgets for the coming year.

Adapting the Planning System. There are numerous variants on the annual strategic planning cycle shown in Figure 8.3. Many have emerged from the recognition that a business or product-market strategy does not have to be changed every year, and that an annual planning system can easily deteriorate into a rather sterile and routine seasonal ritual. In the worst case, the process ends up desensitizing management to important strategic developments as they struggle to complete the routine forms before proceeding to the budget planning.

Signs of planning systems that have become routinized, thereby suppressing the creative search for strategic alternatives,[7] are:

- excessive reporting requirements, usually accompanied by ever-larger planning manuals with more and more standard forms to complete,

- undue short-run operational emphasis, as plans tend to contain primarily operational information and issues, and serve as a basis for budgeting decisions. As a result, internal considerations are given disproportionate weight relative to external forces,

- ineffective use of corporate management time. When each business is required to present the same breadth of analysis during strategy reviews, excessive time is spent on businesses without problems, while those facing serious challenges are inevitably shortchanged,

- isolation of corporate planning staff from operations. The most unproductive relationship occurs when the corporate planning office receives all the business and functional plans at one time, and is required to consolidate and analyze the proposals prior to the strategy review session. If they have previously been isolated from the business units because corporate management was not involved in an ongoing dialogue on strategies and objectives, they have great difficulty giving meaningful responses. The best that such planners can do is search for omissions, invalid assumptions, and other flaws,

- imbalance of advocacy versus consensus. A familiar situation in many companies is the "challenge" review session, during which the corporate staff seemingly tries to shoot down the proposals of the business units while corporate management presides as combination referee and judge. As a consequence, operating management become committed advocates of a preferred option, which they endeavor to sell to senior management in advance of the strategy review. Once a top manager is perceived to have taken a position, other line managers and staff will be unlikely to dissent strongly.

---

7. Rijvnis and Sharman (1982).

An increasingly popular solution to many of these problems is to build more flexibility into the planning system by limiting the full-scale strategy analysis and review to businesses that are clearly in trouble with their current strategy or are facing major opportunities that could transform the basic character. This would be a *maxi-review* and would follow the "A" path in Figure 8.3. For the other businesses that are still in the midst of implementing a shift in strategy or are judged to have an effective strategy, it is sufficient to bypass the first cycle of the planning system for that year. The planning effort for businesses in the "B" category would focus on a few key issues that might require an adjustment in the strategy or might be aimed at advancing a major decision from a previous planning effort, such as launching a new product. Such businesses would undergo a *mini-review* that would focus on the continuing validity of the present strategy and the response to the key issues.

Annual Marketing or Product Plans

For many companies, the annual marketing or product plan remains the focal point of formal strategic planning activity. Increasingly, however, the annual marketing plan is being either absorbed by the strategic business or market plan or assigned a more limited role as a supporting tactical plan. The significance of this supporting role varies widely between companies and industries. Within "market needs" driven companies, in which segmentation and positioning are critical issues, and advertising and promotion represent both a significant proportion of the budget and a major source of competitive advantage, the annual marketing plan is still the most important activity for a product manager. While these annual plans must be closely integrated with the strategic market plan and must support the basic strategic thrust, they still have a number of distinct elements. This is especially true of consumer packaged goods companies that offer a number of brands or products to the same market. A good illustration of the scope of these plans can be found in the following boxed insert, which describes the outline of an annual brand marketing plan in the Scott Paper Company.

A recent study[8] of annual planning practices among companies selling food or health-care products found that the most profitable companies—and by inference, the most effectively managed—were also the most thorough planners.

---

8. Stasch and Lanktree (1980).

Annual Brand Marketing Plan *
Scott Paper Company

I. Category Overview

A summary overview designed to describe category direction, which will position the individual brand marketing discussions that follow. Items to be discussed are:

A. Marketing Objective Summary (volume, share, and share of segment)

B. Financial Goals (margin, earnings contribution, ROI)

C. Key Strategies and Implementation Plan (note if change from prior years)
- Product
- Development and evaluation
- Merchandising and spending
- Pricing

D. Rationale for the above (to support how brands will be differentiated)
- Market size and growth. Segment trends.
- Scott/competitive volume, share, and A & P.
- Scott and competition. Product comparability.
- Test data. Key learning.
- Other observations. Future considerations.

E. Key Issues/Action Plan

II. Brand Marketing Plans

A. *Background*—a brief discussion (three to four paragraphs) of the key factors that drive next year's marketing plan, including:
- Brand history. Repositioning.
- Market/competitive trends.
- Historical marketing support (or lack thereof).
- Relative product quality.

This section would summarize, in a short, relevant fashion, what is included in the business analysis. It is intended to position the document for the reader in a meaningful fashion.

An example: Historically, Brand X was considered to be a declining brand, vulnerable to rollouts of new high-quality base sheets and incapable of maintaining share or volume in the long term. Brand X, however, has demonstrated the ability to maintain volume in the face of these factors. We now believe that Brand X enjoys a unique position in the marketplace, offering the consumer a combination of value and price that is perceived to be superior to alternatives. The plan that follows calls for strengthening this position in current markets and expanding the Brand X offering to other markets, thereby increasing both share and volume.

A key portion of this background section is a discussion regarding "status of implementing current year plan."

B. *Marketing Objectives*—a description of the key marketing accomplishments anticipated next year, with a comparison of these objectives with historical trends
  - volume
  - share (total market)
  - share of relevant segment

C. *Financial Objectives* (including comparison with historical trends)
  - gross margin (%)
  - gross profit after advertising and promotion
  - division earning contribution (%, per case, and total $)

D. *Strategies/Product Positioning Statement*—Explain all marketing strategies being used to achieve the objectives; describe those that are essential to success as thoroughly as possible. For example, if product is a key strategic element in achieving objectives, then product goals must specifically be described even to the extent of enumerating preference levels that are necessary. Other key strategies may be gross profit, pricing, promotion, advertising, distribution, etc. They will vary by brand.

E. *Key Accomplishments/Learning*—Describe the major accomplishments that are expected/necessary over a two-year time horizon in order for the brand or venture to move toward or achieve its objectives. If share-level capability, a cost of sales target, process demonstration, or achievement of product attributes are key accomplishments, then they must be highlighted in this section.

Key Events—Describe those specific events that are directed toward the key accomplishments outlined above, e.g., a predictive product test that is designed to establish the share capability of a particular product/pricing strategy.

F. *Advertising and Promotion Justification*—A & P trends in advertising, consumer, and trade spending should be explained on a year-to-year basis relative to marketing strategy.

A & P levels should be explained as they relate to (1) marketing strategy, (2) competitive spending (total A & P as well as trade rates),

and (3) advertising and promotion strategies. Indicate significant differences in regional spending.

Specifics of the Programming Documents and Media Plans will be
included as Appendixes.

G. *Development Plan*—Describe the objective of any development spending
as it relates to (1) product attribute or cost savings desired and (2)
brand positioning and strategy. State what is expected to result during
the time horizon of the plan, and describe how spending in marketing,
R & D, market research, and engineering supports the goal.

H. *Sensitivities*—In this section, we want to describe those things that have
the capability to affect or change the plan. These sensitivities can be
both external (such as new information or competitive behavior, etc.)
and internal (a management decision, staffing, etc.). It is important
that these sensitivities be highlighted so that in proposing our plan to
management, we do not make promises we cannot keep when we know
that something exists that can critically affect plan accomplishment.

We also want to describe what the potential effect on our plans will
be if the sensitivity occurs. In other words, "Do we have a contingency plan?" These should be discussed in detail at this point.

III. *Summary*—This part of the plan will be a more graphic representation of
key activities as noted above. It should be as specific as possible for a
two-year time horizon. On it should be indicated:

- key accomplishments (both marketing and technical)
- key events (both marketing and technical)
- key decision or resourcing dates or both
- timing of sensitivities
- operating dollar flow
- capital appropriation/expenditures (where applicable)
- alternative or contingency activities

* Adapted from a plan outline appearing in Hopkins (1981).

The best company in the sample used a four-stage process to develop the annual plan for each of the separately
managed brands:

- Starting at weeks 48–22 of the plan development
  period, the product manager reviewed results from
  the semiannual survey of product users and met
  with media and research specialists. The purpose of
  this activity was to identify the tactical alternatives
  to be considered.

- During weeks 20–16, a list of issues facing the
  brand was developed. The marketing director then
  selected the "key issues" to be developed in the
  marketing plan for the next year to keep this plan
  in harmony with the overall strategic plan. At the
  same time, the objectives to be achieved by the plan
  were assigned.

- Weeks 16–8 were used to obtain reactions to the
  evolving marketing plan from various internal and
  external specialists, including a national sales force
  representative who was assigned as liaison to the
  product group.

- During the weeks 10–4, drafts of the marketing
  plan were reviewed with the marketing director and
  other senior management, and were modified to
  reflect their suggestions.

- By week 0, when the plan was formally presented
  to the general manager of the division, few changes
  were likely to be required.

The quality of annual marketing planning in this company was judged to be enhanced by four features of the organization. First, there was a short "chain of command."
The product manager responsible for the plan reported
directly to the marketing director, who in turn reported to
the division general manager. Second, emphasis on training
was strong—managers at every level were expected to train
their immediate subordinates. Third, the dissemination of
planning ideas was encouraged by transferring experienced
personnel between divisions. Last, all members of the product management group were eligible for large bonuses

based on annual divisional profitability in excess of objectives and how well the individual was rated by his or her superiors.

Retaining Flexibility

Strategies are constructed in ambiguous environments in which many significant events cannot be forecast and planned for in their entirety. Some events will not even have been contemplated when the strategy is chosen. The challenge is to design the business strategy in enough detail to ensure consistency of organization approach in coping with the environment while avoiding overspecificity that would impair effective response to unexpected or low-probability events, such as are described in Table 8.3.

Three approaches can be employed to prepare the organization to deal strategically with these events rather than to react in an ad hoc fashion.

Contingency Planning. Contingency plans are a useful device for dealing with risks and opportunities that are not completely unforeseen, but were initially judged to have a low likelihood of occurrence. Procedures for preparing plans for monitoring and responding to risk factors are described in Chapter 6.

Table 8.3 Adapting Plans to Events

THE STRATEGIC PLAN	THE UNEXPECTED EVENT
▪ Product A will be the major source of long-run growth	→ ▪ Raw materials price increases make product A uneconomical
▪ Follow the lead of the major competitor on pricing of product B	→ ▪ Major competitor discontinues product B
▪ Phase out production of product B within two years	
▪ Negotiate a 60/40 joint venture with a small microprocessor company with excellent manufacturing capabilities	→ ▪ An attractive acquisition candidate is available

Build Flexibility into Action Plans. Several steps can be taken to overcome the impression that strategic plans are fixed commitments with an irreversible logic and momentum.[9] One step is to gear the plan to events rather than to the calendar. When resources are committed on the basis of a certain amount next year, another amount the following year, and so on, the plan becomes excessively rigid. This result can be avoided if expenditures, such as plant construction, depend on events such as acceptable performance of the new product in usage tests. At the same time, expenditure plans should be designed so major, irreversible commitments are avoided or delayed as long as possible. Thus, when uncertainty is considerable in demand forecasts, it is prudent to construct smaller-than-optimum plants, which can steadily be expanded as demand develops, rather than a single large plant.

Assess Unexpected Events in Light of Planning Assumptions. In the case of the business planning to negotiate a 60/40 joint venture with a small microprocessor manufacturer, the first step is to return to the logic that led to the strategic choice and test whether the assumptions are still valid. This approach is shown in Table 8.4.

Table 8.4 Assessing Unexpected Events in Light of Planning Assumptions

ORIGINAL ASSUMPTIONS	CURRENT SITUATION	SHOULD WE ACQUIRE?		
		yes	maybe	no
Key product functions will increasingly be provided by microprocessor controls	Still true	✓		
No time is available to develop an internal capability with the new technology	Less urgency because high costs have slowed acceptance		✓	
Joint ventures less risky than acquisitions	No change			✓
We are good at marketing but lack manufacturing capability	So is the acquisition candidate			✓
Acquisition may be too much to digest	More than over with departure of key manager			✓

---

9. Paul, Donovan, and Taylor (1978).

The aquisition opportunity can then be objectively assessed in the context of the overall strategy rather than as a discrete opportunity to be considered solely on its own merits. Clearly, the acquisition candidate does not fit the strategic direction of the business and should not be pursued.

Summary: *Completing the Process*

Implementation signals the conclusion of the planning process; strategic decisions have been converted into action programs, budgets, resource allocations, and period plans with specific tasks, deadlines, and assigned responsibilities. This is a critical stage, for as Drucker [10] reminds us:

> The best plan is only a plan, that is, good intentions, unless it *degenerates into work*. The distinction that makes a plan capable of producing results is the commitment of key people to work on specific tasks.

This chapter has examined a number of elements of strategy implementation, including different approaches to programming, the structure and content of plans, and the planning system that facilitates the dialogue among levels of management. A flexible three-cycle approach was described as generally applicable to business unit planning. Cycle I begins with broad corporate guidelines, Cycle II involves the negotiation of objectives and strategy between corporate- and business-level management, and Cycle III incorporates the final strategy review and the decisions that determine the annual plans.

Planning is a living, adapting, and ongoing activity. Thus, the end of one complete planning process, embracing the iterative steps from situation assessment to strategy evaluation, choice, and implementation, often signals the first cycle of the next complete process. The timing of the next full-scale strategy review will depend on the circumstances of the business unit and the time required to execute the planned programs.

During the interval when no formal planning activity is happening, the business must have a monitoring and control system to establish whether the strategy is delivering the promised objectives and whether the assumptions underlying the strategy are still valid.

---

10. Drucker (1974).

The basis of this system is performance criteria and measures that are derived from the objectives and the key success requirements. For example, if the strategy requires new distribution methods, an inventory control system would be a high priority. It would be used to ensure that inventory levels at various stages were not excessive and likely to back up in the system, or if they were, warning of the need for corrective action would be ample. If too many departures from the expected are identified by the control system, however, it may be necessary to initiate a complete strategy review or a specific issue analysis. Thus, the process begins anew.

Summary: Meeting the Challenges of Strategic Market Planning

Chapter **9**

Many companies have been sorely disappointed with the results of ambitious strategic planning efforts. By some estimates, as few as 10 percent of U.S. companies use strategic planning effectively. In a 1980 survey of 145 planning professionals,[1] 90 percent of the sample admitted their strategies were not being effectively implemented and thus were not having a material impact on company performance.

These unsatisfactory results are not surprising, for there are many pitfalls to overcome. Some stem from poor management of the planning process, including unclear direction from corporate management, overemphasis on short-run financial consequences, and ineffective review and integration of plans. These problems are compounded by the lack of development of organization, management selection, and reward systems to support the strategy. Other problems stem from the tendency to resist the changes in the status quo that planning implicitly encourages. Planning can also create enormous stress within an organization, especially when individual roles are not well defined or when participants in the process cannot determine what is expected of them.

Underlying the disappointments and pitfalls are four fundamental challenges, each representing a major theme that has been woven through this book:

- achieving an external orientation so there is continual pursuit of new sources of competitive advantage within the markets the business elects to serve,

Fix your eyes on the stars but beware of the potholes in the ground lest you stumble on the road to destiny.

—Greek Philosopher

---

1. Allen (1980).

- building a commitment to planning through functional management involvement in the planning process,

- fostering rather than stunting creativity, and

- ensuring a capability exists to adapt effectively to unfolding events.

The purpose of this chapter is to highlight these four themes as a basis for discussing how to get the maximum benefits from strategic market planning.

Achieving an External Orientation

Effective business strategies share many characteristics, but at a minimum, they are close to the marketplace, exploit the competencies of the organization, and employ valid assumptions about environment trends and competitive behavior. Above all, they must offer a realistic basis for gaining and sustaining a competitive advantage. These criteria—of validity and reality—are pivotal during the strategy evaluation phase of the planning process. The testing of strategies cannot stop here, however. Competitors' actions and changes in the marketplace deliberately conspire to erode the basis for advantage. Thus, it is essential that all functions understand the present sources of advantage and continually work together to find new sources of advantage in anticipation of the inevitable erosion.

The necessity for such an external orientation is further emphasized in the findings of Peters and Waterman [2] on the characteristics of excellent companies. In all these companies, closeness to the customer is sought and nurtured with unusual intensity. This orientation, however, does not start and stop at the point of contact with the customer; it pervades all levels of the organization and shapes the assumptions about what issues are critical.

An important feature of an effective external orientation is continual questioning and monitoring of environmental assumptions. It is easy to forget that strategic decisions involve uncertainty and that the assumptions made to cope with this uncertainty have a significant probability of being wrong. Instead, the assumptions are codified and quantified into precise three- or five-year forecasts of market growth, market share, and profit margins that communicate

---

2. Peters and Waterman (1982).

far more certainty about the future than is warranted. To counter-
act this false impression, it is important to check assumptions continually to make sure they are still valid. This requires an information
system that is designed to monitor the environment and not just
provide the readily available measures of performance. Equally
important, it means a willingness to tolerate uncertainty and learn
from it—to be error embracing rather than error denying. Indeed,
a persuasive point of view holds that strategic planning is most
effective when it sensitizes management to important trends and
changes in assumptions so they are equipped to monitor and
respond faster than the competition.

The Strategic Role of Marketing

A distinction is sometimes made between how "the matter of
strategy making is approached [strategic management] and how
strategy usage is conducted [operations management]." [3] This view
unnecessarily discounts the need for strategic thinking at the product-market level of the business and undermines the critical role of a
marketing orientation within strategic planning. An alternative
perspective, which accords a strategic role to marketing within
product-markets and business units, is that the primary concern of
strategic management should be the formulation and implementation of corporate-level strategy. Within diversified firms, this
encompasses:

- the *organizational context* of strategic decisions and the relationship of strategy and organizational structure,

- the strategic *decision processes,* including formal systems for
  planning, implementing, and controlling,

- the specific *resource allocations* to existing businesses or major
  growth ventures.

Marketing can contribute to creative thinking within each of
these areas, especially to decision process and resource allocation
questions. The fundamental reason is that the appropriate level of
analysis for addressing these two areas is more likely to be the individual product-market or business unit, and not the firm as a whole.
Inevitably, a corporate or "top-down" perspective can be only partially informed about the threats and opportunities at this level of
competitive interaction and the specific details of the company's

---

3. Schendel (1982).

relationship with their customers and distribution channels. Therefore, the strategic decision process requires a dialogue about individual strategies based on the specifics of market segments and competitive positions.

Building Commitment

Strategic planning means change, and change will be resisted unless it is evident that senior management is supportive of the planning activity and that line management has participated actively in the choice of the new directions. Otherwise, the management will not devote their energy to creating effective strategies or to achieving a level of understanding and consensus sufficient to focus attention.

The overriding requirement for organizational commitment is strong support by senior management—both at the corporate and at the division general management levels. It is their behavior that counts, for this is what sends signals to the other levels of management about what is expected. If they do not appear to take planning seriously, neither will the rest of the organization.

Equally essential to a meaningful commitment to strategic planning is the active involvement of all levels of management in the planning process. Without broad participation, it is likely that essential information about opportunities, capabilities, and market responses will be overlooked. The information and experience of line management are of little value unless they can be incorporated into the strategic thinking process at the time when critical judgments and assumptions are being made. Second, the effectiveness of a strategy depends on consistency of action and congruency of the programs undertaken by functional groups or program managers. Assurance of such consistency is much greater when there is a shared understanding of the assumptions, premises, and expected results that underlie the chosen strategy. This sharing of perspectives requires a forum for dialogue and debate in which problems can be aired, assumptions can be challenged, and opportunities can be examined from a variety of functional perspectives. Finally, active involvement by operating management yields greater commitment to implementing the strategy. Both field and laboratory studies [4] have found that "self-set" objectives are more motivating

---

4. Bass (1977) and French, Kay, and Meyer (1966).

The Five Most Serious Planning Pitfalls to be Avoided

1. Top management's assumption that it can delegate the planning function to a planner.

2. Top management becomes so engrossed in current problems that it spends insufficient time on long-range planning, and the process becomes discredited among other managers and staff.

3. Failure to develop company goals as a basis for formulating long-range plans.

4. Failure to assure the necessary involvement in the planning process of major line personnel.

5. Failing to use plans as standards for measuring managerial performance.

---

than objectives set by others. Indeed, if planning is perceived simply as a device to control line management, its impact may be even detrimental.

Planners Do Not Plan—They Help Management Plan!

The abstract virtues of strong and continuing senior management support and line management participation are often forgotten in the pressure of daily events and the tyranny of quarterly earnings and performance reviews. Consequently, senior management is often tempted to take shortcuts by delegating planning to the planning staff or retaining outside consultants to prepare the plan. While these steps promise short-run relief from the discipline and time demands of the strategic planning process, they usually compound the problem in the long run. An indication of the prevalence of this type of mistake comes from a survey by Steiner.[5] He asked a sample of planners and managers from 215 firms to choose the top five planning problems they had encountered from a list of fifty possible pitfalls (see boxed insert).

Planning staff and outside consultants can make a significant contribution to the quality of the planning activities, so long as it is

---

5. Steiner (1979).

recognized that they play a supportive and facilitating role. This may include conducting special market and financial analyses, gathering and analyzing competitive data, exploring the implications of strategic options, and preparing position papers on significant issues. They cannot take responsibility for the content of the business strategy, however. This responsibility must be assumed by those accountable for the execution of the strategy. Companies are increasingly turning to strategic *profiling* approaches to overcome these problems and to integrate staff and line management perspectives.

Strategic Profiling: A Flexible Planning Approach

Profiling is a term usually attributed to the consulting firm Arthur D. Little to describe:

> . . . a *thorough assessment* (profile) of the current situation of a strategic business unit and the prospects for strategic redirection,

> . . . undertaken collectively by the *management team,*

> . . . following the sequence of steps in the strategic *planning process.*

The profiling sessions, with the management team as participants, should be led by someone from outside the business unit being profiled. This person need not be from outside the company, but should not be there as a symbol of hierarchical authority. What is needed is intelligent naivete about the unit, coupled with a thorough familiarity with strategic planning processes and methods, and experience in leading meetings.

The first profiling session is usually a two- or three-day affair, devoted to assembling available information and judgments, and organizing this background so it is useful for formulating and evaluating strategies. The session participants include all those with responsibility for deciding on and implementing any change in strategic direction, as well as members of the planning staff at divisional or corporate level. During the first session, relevant information and judgments on the current strategy and elements of the situation are recorded on presentation sheets. Preliminary identification of critical issues and strategic options is then derived from this information. At the end of the session, specific analysis tasks are assigned to members of the management team. The priorities to be assigned to these tasks usually depend on how critical the information is to an understanding of the current and prospective situation of the business unit or business segment. This may be as basic as the determination of the potential size of an attractive market segment or the profitability consequences of the momentum of the present strategy.

Further profiling sessions will be held to monitor progress in assembling information and refining the strategy options. In all sessions, full participation of operating management is encouraged to ensure that major issues and assumptions are fully understood. A final profiling session will be devoted to a thorough evaluation of the two or three key options and to arriving at a tentative decision as to which one is to be recommended to corporate management.

The advantages of the profiling approach are first that it can readily be adapted to the idiosyncrasies of a corporate culture as well as to differences among business units. Second, the profiling approach brings planners into regular contact with line management and encourages a relationship of cooperation toward a common goal. Third, the managers employ the planning tools and concepts themselves while drawing on the resources and experience of the outside facilitator to ensure the tools and concepts are properly interpreted and applied. Finally, both the process and the outcomes are readily accepted by operating managers who appreciate the underlying premise of the profiling approach; that is, they know what they are doing with their business better than anyone else and have the responsibility for formulating their own strategy options.

Fostering Creativity

Concern is growing that strategic planning—especially as practiced in many large companies—is restraining creativity and slowing response to emerging threats and opportunities. One argument is that strategic concepts and analytical methods focus attention on a few key variables at the expense of peripheral vision.[6] It is said that Japanese managers regard a propensity to be guided by "strategic formulas" as a weakness. In their judgment, it is peripheral vision that picks up changes in the customer or technology or competition, and so is the key to corporate survival over the long haul. Another concern is that formalized and systematized approaches to strategic planning have a tendency to become routinized, procedural activi-

---

6. Pascale (1982).

ties in which the emphasis is on form rather than on substance. Lengthy standard planning forms also lack impact. They are often too long for senior management to read, absorb, and pass judgment on. Hence, at the end of the planning cycle, operating managers heave a sigh of relief and say, "Thank heavens that's over. Now we can get back to running the business."

Yet, as one company attests, planning can also enhance creativity (see boxed insert).

How can the benefits of strategic planning be retained without the loss of creativity and the essential marketing orientation? Most suggestions for improvement have been directed at the design and implementation of the planning system and procedures. Experience has indicated, for example, that it is desirable to (1) avoid premature closure on one preferred strategic option, (2) keep the planning procedures simple at the outset and add complexity only when the organization is ready, (3) build flexibility into the planning system by limiting the full-scale strategy analysis to a subset of all businesses, as described in Chapter 8, and (4) tailor the planning approach to the characteristics of the key people. For instance, some senior executives prefer substantial written support for all major decisions, while others prefer terse oral summaries. In gen-

---

One Management's View of Planning

- Planning will not give you a "perfect crystal ball," nor will it enable you to predict the future with extreme accuracy.

- Planning will not necessarily prevent you from making mistakes.

- Planning will or should minimize the degree to which you are taken by surprise and help you revise both programs and activities whenever it is desirable to do so. In other words, planning will help you react creatively to change.

- Planning will result in the integration of all of the company's activities and maximize your efforts toward the attainment of corporate goals.

- Planning does not stifle creativity. Planning *enhances* creativity by creating orderly processes whereby viable objectives and plans can be reached.

Source: *Guide to Preparing Marketing Plans*, Litton Group, quoted in Hopkins (1981).

eral, it is preferable to communicate as much preliminary thinking as possible verbally during profiling sessions rather than by prior memoranda, in order to fit the natural style of most managers. Eventually, it is necessary to undertake the discipline of summarizing the key elements of the strategy options in writing, but not before the broad shape has been widely discussed among the management team.

In summary, creativity is best served when an open dialogue exists among the various decision-making levels in the organization about the key issues facing the business, and operating managers are rewarded for thinking and acting strategically.

Ensuring Adaptability

Two different frameworks for thinking about how things get done in organizations are broadly classed as *Down and Out* and *Up and In.*[7] We have already encountered these two orientations in earlier chapters of this book in the contrast of top-down versus bottom-up perspectives on market analysis (in Chapter 4) and strategic planning systems (in Chapter 8).

The *Down and Out* view is "dominated by the seldom questioned logic of sequential decision steps and belief systems that accept as axiomatic the downward flow of organizational authority." The processes of deciding on strategy and of implementing the strategy are distinctly separated, with overtones that those who decide are to be different from those who implement. For advocates of this approach to planning, the quality of decision is paramount; "without a high quality decision to implement, effective implementation isn't worth much." By contrast, "the *Up and In* perspective's essential normative proposition is that decision making and implementation ought to be interwoven and interactive. The core context of thought focuses on the emotional nature of man." There is a distinct preference for muddling through, cut-and-try processes that are opportunistic and adaptive. The essence of this perspective is that commitment and acceptance are essential to effective implementation; therefore, the people whose support is required must be involved in the process of deciding.

---

7. Leavitt and Webb (1978).

These two orientations are seldom encountered as polarities. Indeed, each is partially embedded in the other, with the weakness of one often being the strength of the other, thus creating the need for careful balancing of perspectives. As we have seen, this notion is applicable to most areas of planning. For example, the benefits of a balanced view were the basis for concluding that while the "top-down" or industry perspective on market definitions was different from the customer perspective, the two were not competitive and should be used together to guide complementary insights. Similarly, an integrated, multicycle planning system with continuing dialogue among levels of management is generally superior to either a purely top-down or a bottom-up planning system.

The most striking parallel with these two views about decision making is found in the distinction between strategies that evolve incrementally and those developed in the course of a formal planning process. Our emphasis in this book has been on the latter; indeed, the book is organized to follow the steps of such a process. Equally effective strategies may emerge from continual adaptation to unfolding events. According to field studies of this adaptation, the process begins with the conscious selection of product/market/ technology segments that the business could dominate given its resource limits. Executives then "proceed incrementally to handle urgent matters, to start long term sequences whose specific future branches and consequences were perhaps murky, to respond to unforeseen events as they occurred, to build on successes, and to brace up or cut losses on failures." [8]

One of the roles of formal planning within this incremental, adaptive process is to serve as a trigger to strategic change, usually by stimulating longer term studies. Such changes, however, could also come through precipitating events and subsystem planning within functional areas. From this perspective, formal strategic decision-making processes as well as annual planning activities are simply one means to an end. In reality, that "end game" is never reached, for good strategies are continually evolving and adapting. For this adaptation to be successful, however, the emerging strategy must continually be tested against the criteria of validity and reality.

In summary, businesses are best served by strategies that provide a broad game plan for competing for advantage within the markets the business elects to serve, while leaving the details of carrying out the specific plays—the tactical actions—to a management team with a commitment to that strategy.

---

8. Quinn (1981).

Bibliography

Abell, Derek F. "Strategic Windows." *Journal of Marketing* 42 (July 1978): 21–26.

Abell, Derek F. *Defining the Business: The Starting Point of Strategic Planning.* Englewood Cliffs, N.J.: Prentice-Hall, 1980.

Abell, Derek F., and John S. Hammond. *Strategic Market Planning: Problems and Analytical Approaches.* Englewood Cliffs, N.J.: Prentice-Hall, 1979.

Allen, Michael. "The Corporate Strategy Gaps." *Management Today* (September 1980): 108–13.

Andrews, Kenneth. *The Concept of Corporate Strategy.* Homewood, Ill.: Dow-Jones-Irwin, 1971.

Ansoff, H. Igor. *Corporate Strategy.* New York: McGraw-Hill, 1965.

Ansoff, H. Igor. "Strategic Issue Management." *Strategic Management Journal* (1980): 131–48.

Armstrong, J. Scott. "The Value of Formal Planning for Strategic Decisions: Review of Evidence." *Strategic Management Journal* (forthcoming 1982).

Bales, Carter F. "Strategic Control: The President's Paradox." *Business Horizons* (August 1977): 17–28.

Barabba, Vincent. "Research Process Helps Marketing Executives Fine-Tune Strategic Plans." *Marketing News* (18 September 1981): 12.

Bass, Bernard M. "Utility of Managerial Self-Planning on a Simulated Production Task with Replications in Twelve Countries." *Journal of Applied Psychology* 62 (1977): 506–9.

Becton-Dickinson and Company. Unpublished case series, (A), (B), (C), (D). University of Virginia, 1980.

Bennett, James E. "Why Plan Strategically?" Paper presented to Business Week Strategy Planning Conference, Toronto, Ontario, 10 November 1980.

Bettis, Richard A., and William K. Hall. "Strategic Portfolio Management in the Multi-Business Firm." *California Management Review* 24 (Fall 1981): 23–38.

Bierman, Harold, Jr. *Strategic Financial Planning: A Manager's Guide to Improving Profit Performance.* New York: Free Press, 1980.

Boyd, Harper W., Jr., and Jean-Claude Larreché. "The Foundations of Marketing Strategy." In *Annual Review of Marketing, 1978,* edited by Gerald Zaltman and Thomas Bonoma, 41–72. Chicago: American Marketing Association, 1978.

Business Week. "New Rivals in Turnkey Systems." (23 June 1980).

———. "When Marketing Failed at Texas Instruments." (22 June 1981): 91–94.

———. "A.O. Smith: 'Safe Diversification That is Endangering Profits.'" (21 September 1981): 82–83.

———. "The Hennessy Style May be What Allied Needs." (11 January 1982).

———. "Hyster: A Top-of-the-Line Producer Tries to Beat Japan at its Own Game." (8 February 1982): 99–100.

———. "Emerson Electric: High Profits from Low Tech." (4 April 1983): 58–62.

———. "Firestone Tries the Service Business Again." (20 June 1983): 70–71.

———. "A British Builder Exports its Blueprint for Affordable Homes." (18 July 1983): 68–69.

———. "Suddenly U.S. Companies Are Teaming Up." (11 July 1983): 71–74.

Buzzell, Robert D. "Competitive Behavior and Product Life Cycles." In *New Ideas for Successful Marketing,* edited by John Wright and Jac Goldstucker. Chicago: American Marketing Association, 1966.

Buzzell, Robert D. *Note on Market Definition and Segmentation.* Cambridge: Harvard Business School, 1979a.

Buzzell, Robert D. "The Dispute About High Share Businesses." *Pimsletter* 19 (1979b). Strategic Planning Institute.

Buzzell, Robert D., and Frederick D. Wiersema. "Successful Share-Building Strategies." *Harvard Business Review* (January–February 1981): 135–44.

Buzzell, Robert D., "Is Vertical Integration Profitable?" *Harvard Business Review* 83 (January–February 1983): 92–102.

Cadbury, N. D. "When, Where and How to Test Market." *Harvard Business Review* (May–June 1975): 96–105.

Caves, Richard E., and Michael E. Porter. "From Entry Barriers to Mobility Barriers: Conjectural Decisions and Contrived Deterrence to New Competition." *Quarterly Journal of Economics* 91 (1977): 241–62.

Charan, Ram. "How to Strengthen Your Strategy Review Process." *Journal of Business Strategy* 2 (Winter 1982): 50–60.

Collier, Don. "Strategic Planning Systems Design and Operation." *Journal of Business Strategy* 1 (Fall 1980): 76–77.

Colvin, Geoffrey. "Federal Express Dives Into Air Mail." *Fortune* (15 June 1981): 106–8.

Corey, E. Raymond. "Key Options in Market Selection and Product Planning." *Harvard Business Review* (September–October 1975): 118–24.

Cosier, R. A., and J. C. Aplin. "A Critical View of Dialectical Inquiry as a Tool in Strategic Planning." *Strategic Management Journal* 1 (October–November 1980): 343–56.

Cushman, Robert. "Corporate Strategy: Planning for the Future." Paper presented to the North American Society of Corporate Planners, Boston, 19 October 1978.

Cushman, Robert. "Norton's Top-Down, Bottom-Up Planning Process." *Planning Review* (November 1979): 3–8, 48.

Day, George. "Diagnosing the Product Portfolio." *Journal of Marketing* (April 1977): 29–38.

Day, George S. "Strategic Market Analysis and Definition: An Integrated Approach." *Strategic Management Journal* (July–September 1981): 281–301.

Day, George S. "Product Life Cycles: Analysis and Applications." *Journal of Marketing* (Fall 1981).

Day, George S., Allan D. Shocker, and Rajendra K. Srivastava. "Customer-Oriented Approaches to Identifying Product-Markets." *Journal of Marketing* 43 (Fall 1979): 8–19.

Dreyfuss, Joel. "Smithkline's Ulcer Medicine 'Holy War.'" *Fortune* (19 September 1983): 129–36.

Drucker, Peter F. *Management: Tasks, Responsibilities, Practices.* New York: Harper & Row, 1974.

Drucker, Peter F. *Managing in Turbulent Times.* New York: Harper & Row, 1980.

Emshoff, James R., and Arthur Finnel. "Defining Corporate Strategy: A Case Study Using Strategic Assumptions Analysis." *Sloan Management Review* (Spring 1979): 41–52.

Epstein, Barbara. "Competition and Innovation in Electrical Transmission Equipment." *Industrial Marketing Management* 7 (1978): 9–16.

Fogg, C. Davis. "Anticipate Market Changes, Redefine Business and Readjust Strategic Mix to Ensure Long-Term Success." *Marketing News* (18 March 1983): 2–16.

Forbis, John L., and Nitin T. Mehta. "Value-Based Strategies for Industrial Products." *Business Horizons* (Summer 1982): 32–42.

Frederick, Glenn D. "Relating Environmental Analysis to Corporate Objectives: The Survival Question Technique." Working paper (November 1982).

French, John, E. Kay, and H. H. Meyer. "Participation and the Appraisal System." *Human Relations* 19 (1966): 3–20.

Galbraith, Jay R., and Daniel A. Nathanson. *Strategy Implementation: The Role of Structure and Process.* St. Paul: West Publishing, 1978.

Garda, Robert A. "Strategic Segmentation: How to Carve Niches for Growth in Industrial Markets." *Management Review* (August 1981): 15–22.

Gardner, David M., and Howard Thomas. "Strategic Marketing: History, Issues and Emergent Themes." In *Strategic Marketing and Management.* New York: John Wiley, 1983.

Gluck, Frederick W., Richard N. Foster, and John L. Forbis. "Cure for Strategic Malnutrition." *Harvard Business Review* (November–December 1976): 154–65.

Gluck, Frederick W., Stephen P. Kaufman, and A. Steven Walleck. "Strategic Management for Competitive Advantage." *Harvard Business Review* (July–August 1980): 154–61.

Grant, John H., and William R. King. *The Logic of Strategic Planning.* Boston: Little, Brown, 1982.

Hall, William K. "SBUs: Hot, New Topic in the Management of Diversification." *Business Horizons* (February 1978): 17–25.

Hall, William K. "Survival Strategies in a Hostile Environment." *Harvard Business Review* 58 (September–October 1980): 75–85.

Hamermesh, Richard. "Administrative Issues Posed by Contemporary Approaches to Strategic Planning: The Case of the Dexter Corporation." Working paper, Harvard Business School, 1979.

Hamermesh, R. G., M. J. Anderson, Jr., and J. E. Harris. "Strategies for Low Market Share Businesses." *Harvard Business Review* 56 (May–June 1978): 95–102.

Hartman, Curtis. "PBA: A Tale of Two Airlines." *Inc.* (February 1983).

Haspeslagh, Philippe. "Portfolio Planning: Uses and Limits." *Harvard Business Review* 60 (January–February 1982): 59–73.

Hayes, Robert H., and William J. Abernathy. "Managing Our Way to Economic Decline." *Harvard Business Review* (July–August 1980): 67–77.

Hayes, Robert H., and David A. Garvin. "Managing as if Tomorrow Mattered." *Harvard Business Review* 60 (May–June 1982): 70–79.

Hedley, Barry. "A Fundamental Approach to Strategy Development." *Long Range Planning* (December 1976).

Hedley, Barry. "Strategy and the Business Portfolio." *Long Range Planning* 10 (February 1977): 9–15.

Heenan, David A., and Robert B. Addleman. "Quantitative Techniques for Today's Decision Makers." *Harvard Business Review* (May–June 1976).

Henderson, Bruce D. *Henderson on Corporate Strategy.* Cambridge, Mass.: Abt Books, 1979.

Higgins, Robert C. "How Much Growth Can a Firm Afford?" *Financial Management* 6 (Fall 1977): 7–16.

Hobbs, John M., and Donald F. Heaney. "Coupling Strategy to Operating Plans." *Harvard Business Review* (May–June 1977): 119–26.

Hofer, Charles W. "Toward a Contingency Theory of Business Strategy." *Academy of Management Journal* 18 (December 1975): 784–810.

Hofer, Charles W. "Turnaround Strategies." *The Journal of Business* Strategy 1 (Summer 1980): 19–31.

Hofer, Charles W., and Dan Schendel. *Strategy Formulation: Analytical Concepts.* St. Paul: West Publishing, 1978.

Hogarth, Robin M., and Spyros Makridakis. "Forecasting and Planning: An Evaluation." *Management Science* 27 (February 1981): 115–38.

Holloway, Clark, and William R. King. "Evaluating Alternative Approaches to Strategic Planning." *Long Range Planning* 12 (August 1979): 74–78.

Hopkins, David S. *The Marketing Plan.* New York: Conference Board, 1981.

Hunsicker, J. Q. "Can Top Managers be Strategists?" *Strategic Management Journal* 1 (January–March 1980): 77–84.

Hunsicker, J. Quincy. "The Malaise of Strategic Planning." *The McKinsey Quarterly* (Spring 1980): 2–12.

Hunt, Michael S. "Competition in the Major Home Appliance Industry: 1960–1970." Ph.D. diss., Harvard University, 1972.

Johnson, William E. "Trade-Offs in Pricing Strategy." In *Pricing Practices and Strategies.* New York: Conference Board, 1978.

Kiechel, Walter. "Three (or Four, or More) Ways to Win." *Fortune* (19 October 1981): 181–84.

Kiechel, Walter. "Playing By the Rules of the Corporate Strategy Game." *Fortune* (24 September 1979): 110–15

Keller, George. *Academic Strategy: The Management Revolution in American Higher Education.* Baltimore: Johns Hopkins University Press, 1983.

King, William R. "The Importance of Strategic Issues." *Journal of Business Strategy* 1 (Winter 1981): 74–76.

Kotler, Philip. "Harvesting Strategies for Weak Products." *Business Horizons* 21 (August 1978): 17–22.

Kotler, Philip. *Marketing Management: Analysis, Planning and Control.* 4th ed. Englewood Cliffs, N.J.: Prentice-Hall, 1980.

Kotler, Philip, and Ravi Singh. "Marketing Warfare in the 1980s." *Journal of Business Strategy* 1 (Winter 1981): 30–41.

Kuczmarski, Thomas D., and Steven J. Silver. "Strategy: The Key to Successful New Product Development." *Management Review* (July 1982): 26–40.

Leavitt, Harold J., and Eugene J. Webb. "Implementing: Two Approaches." Working paper, Stanford University (March 1978).

Levine, Josh. "Federal Express Fax Service Takes Off." *Advertising Age* (25 May 1981): 6.

Levitt, Theodore. "Marketing Success Through Differentiation—of Anything." *Harvard Business Review* (January–February 1980): 83–92.

Liddell Hart, B. H. *Strategy.* New York: Praeger, 1967.

Lochridge, Richard K. "Strategy in the Eighties." *Annual Perspective.* Boston Consulting Group, 1981.

Loomis, Carol J. "AMF Vrooms into Who Knows What." *Fortune* (9 April 1979): 76–82.

Loomis, Worth. "Strategic Planning in Uncertain Times." *Chief Executive* (Winter 1980–81).

Lorange, Peter. *Corporate Planning: An Executive Viewpoint.* Englewood Cliffs, N.J.: Prentice-Hall, 1980.

Lorange, Peter, and Richard F. Vancil. *Strategic Planning Systems.* Englewood Cliffs, N.J.: Prentice-Hall, 1977.

Loving, Rush. "The Bus Lines are on the Road to Nowhere." *Fortune* (31 December 1978): 58–64.

Lunn, Tony. "Segmenting and Constructing Markets." In *Consumer Market Research Handbook,* edited by R. M. Worcester. London: McGraw-Hill, 1972.

MacMillan, Ian C. "Seizing Competitive Initiative." *Journal of Business Strategy* 2 (Spring 1982): 43–57.

Maier, Norman R. F. *Problem-Solving Discussions and Conferences.* New York: McGraw-Hill, 1963.

Majaro, Simon. "Market Share: Deception or Diagnosis?" *Marketing* (March 1977): 43–47.

Mason, Richard O., and Ian I. Mitroff. *Challenging Strategic Planning Assumptions: Theory, Cases and Techniques.* New York: John Wiley, 1981.

Mason, Richard O., Ian I. Mitroff, and Vincent P. Barabba. "Creating The Manager's Plan Book: A New Route to Effective Planning." *Planning Review* (July 1980): 11–16, 47.

Michael, Donald N. *On Learning to Plan and Planning to Learn.* Boston: Jossey-Bass, 1973.

Moore, Thomas. "Embattled Kodak Enters the Electronic Age." *Fortune* (22 August 1983): 120–28.

Moran, William T. "Research on Discrete Consumption Markets Can Guide Resource Shifts." *Marketing News* (15 May 1981): 4.

Neubauer, F. Friedrich, and Norman B. Solomon. "A Managerial Approach to Environmental Assessment." *Long Range Planning* 10 (April 1977): 12–20.

O'Connor, Rochelle. *Planning Under Uncertainty: Multiple Scenarios and Contingency Planning.* New York: Conference Board, 1978.

Ohmae, Kenichi. *The Mind of the Strategist: The Art of Japanese Business.* New York: McGraw-Hill, 1982.

Oliver, Alex R., and Joseph R. Garber. "Implementing Strategic Planning: Ten Sure-Fire Ways to Do it Wrong." *Business Horizons* (March–April 1983): 49–51.

Palesy, Steven. "Motivating Line Management Using the Planning Process." *Planning Review* (March 1980).

Pascale, Richard T. "Our Curious Addiction to Corporate Grand Strategy." *Fortune* (25 January 1982): 115–16.

Patel, Peter, and Michael Younger. "A Frame of Reference for Strategy Development." *Long Range Planning* 11 (April 1978): 6–12.

Paul, Ronald N., Neil B. Donovan, and James W. Taylor. "The Reality Gap in Strategic Planning." *Harvard Business Review* (May–June 1978): 124–30.

Pekar, Peter P. "The Strategic Environmental Matrix: A Concept on Trial." *Planning Review* (September 1982): 28–30.

Pennington, Malcolm W., and Steve M. Cohen. "Michael Porter Speaks on Strategy." *Planning Review* 10 (January 1982): 8–12, 36–39.

Peters, Thomas J. "Putting Excellence Into Management." *Business Week* (21 July 1980): 196–205.

Peters, Thomas J., and Robert H. Waterman, Jr. *In Search of Excellence: Lessons from America's Best-Run Companies.* New York: Harper & Row, 1982.

Petre, Peter D. "Meet the Lean Mean New IBM." *Fortune* (13 June 1983): 68–78.

Phillips, L. W., D. R. Chang, and R. D. Buzzell. "Product Quality, Cost Position and Business Performance: A Test of Some Key Hypotheses." *Journal of Marketing* 47 (Spring 1983).

Porter, Michael E. "Strategy Under Conditions of Adversity." Discussion paper 77–13, Harvard Business School, May 1977.

Porter, Michael E. "How Competitive Forces Shape Strategy." *Harvard Business Review* (March–April 1979): 137–45.

Porter, Michael E. *Competitive Strategy: Techniques for Analyzing Industries and Competitors.* New York: Free Press, 1980.

Quinn, James Brian. "Strategic Change: Logical Incrementalism." *Sloan Management Review* (Fall 1978): 7–21.

Quinn, James Brian. "Formulating Strategy One Step at a Time." *Journal of Business Strategy* 1 (Winter 1981): 42–63.

Rappaport, Alfred. "Selecting Strategies That Create Shareholder Value." *Harvard Business Review* (May–June 1981): 139–49.

Reece, James S., and William R. Cool. "Measuring Investment Center Performance." *Harvard Business Review* (May–June 1978): 28–30.

Richards, Max D. *Organization Goal Structures.* St. Paul: West Publishing, 1978.

Rijvnis, Arie J., and Grahma J. Sharman. "New Life for Formal Planning Systems." *Journal of Business Strategy* 2 (Spring 1982): 100–105.

Robinson, S.J.Q. "What Growth Rate Can You Achieve?" *Long Range Planning* 12 (August 1979): 7–12.

Robinson, S.J.Q., R. E. Hickens, and D. P. Wade. "The Directional Policy Matrix: Tool for Strategic Planning." *Long Range Planning* 17 (1978): 8–15.

Ross, Joel E., and Michael J. Kami. *Corporations in Crisis: Why the Mighty Fall.* Englewood Cliffs, N.J.: Prentice-Hall, 1973.

Rothschild, William E. *Putting It All Together: A Guide to Strategic Thinking.* New York: AMACON, 1976.

Rothschild, William E. *Strategic Alternatives: Selection, Development and Implementation.* New York: AMACON, 1979.

Rothschild, William E. "How to Ensure the Continued Growth of Strategic Planning." *The Journal of Business Strategy* 1 (Summer 1980): 11–18.

Rudden, Eileen M. "The Misuse of a Sound Investment Tool." *Wall Street Journal* (1 November 1982).

Rumelt, Richard P. "Evaluation of Strategy: Theory and Methods." In *Strategic Management: A New View of Business Policy and Planning,* edited by Dan E. Schendel and Charles W. Hofer. Boston: Little, Brown, 1978.

Rumelt, Richard P. "The Evaluation of Business Strategy." In *Business Policy and Strategic Management,* edited by William F. Glueck, 359–67. 3d ed. New York: McGraw-Hill, 1980.

Schendel, Dan. "Strategic Management and Strategic Marketing: What is Strategic About Either One?" Paper presented at the Strategic Marketing Workshop, University of Illinois, 10–11 May 1982.

Schendel, Dan G., Richard Palton, and James Riggs. "Corporate Turnaround Strategies: A Study of Profit Decline and Recovery." *Journal of General Management* 3 (Spring 1976).

Schoeffler, Sidney. "Capital-Intensive Technology vs. ROI: A Strategic Assessment." *Management Review* (September 1978): 8–14.

Smith, Lee. "Dow vs. DuPont: Rival Formulas for Leadership." *Fortune* (10 September 1979): 74–84.

South, Stephen E. "Competitive Advantage: The Cornerstone of Strategic Thinking." *The Journal of Business Strategy* 1 (Spring 1981): 15–25.

Stasch, Stanley, and Patricia Lanktree. "Can Your Marketing Planning Procedures be Improved?" *Journal of Marketing* 44 (Summer 1980): 79–90.

Steiner, George A. *Strategic Planning: What Every Manager Must Know.* New York: Free Press, 1979.

Stevenson, Howard H. "Defining Strengths and Weaknesses." *Sloan Management Review* 17 (Spring 1976): 51–68.

Struse, R. W. "Marketing Research Can Sharpen Focus on 'Fuzzy' Product Category Definitions." *Marketing News* (15 May 1981): 18.

Stuart, Alexander. "A Pump Maker Primed for Profit." *Fortune* (23 February 1981): 114–20.

Sultan, Ralph G. M. *Pricing in the Electrical Obgopoly.* Vol. I and II. Cambridge: Division of Research, Harvard Graduate School of Business Administration, 1974.

Tilles, Seymour. "How to Evaluate Corporate Strategy." *Harvard Business Review* 41 (July–August 1963): 111–21.

Tilles, Seymour. *Making Strategy Explicit—A Special Commentary.* Boston Consulting Group, 1966.

Tregoe, Benjamin, and John W. Zimmerman. *Top Management Strategy: What it Is and How to Make it Work.* New York: Simon & Schuster, 1980.

Tversky, Amos, and D. Kahneman. "Judgment Under Uncertainty: Heuristics and Biases." *Science* 185 (1974): 1124–31.

Urban, Glen L., and John R. Hauser. *Design and Marketing of New Products.* Englewood Cliffs, N.J.: Prentice-Hall, 1980.

Uttal, Bro. "Texas Instruments Regroups." *Fortune* (9 August 1982): 40–45.

Weber, John A. *Growth Opportunity Analysis.* Reston, Va.: Reston Publishing, 1976.

Welch, John F., Jr. "Where Is Marketing Now That We Really Need It?" Paper presented at the Conference Board's 1981 Marketing Conference, Grant Hyatt, New York City, October 1981.

Wensley, Robin. "Strategic Marketing: Betas, Boxes or Basics." *Journal of Marketing* 45 (Summer 1981): 173–82.

Wheelwright, Steven C., and Robert L. Banks. "Involving Operating Managers in Planning Process Evolution." *Sloan Management Review* (Summer 1979): 43–59.

Wilkinson, George. *Environmental Scanning: How It Can be Used to Support the Long Range Planning Process.* Alexandria, Va.: United Way of America, 1980.

Wind, Yoram. "Issues and Advances in Segmentation Research." *Journal of Marketing Research* 15 (August 1978).

Wind, Yoram, and Vijay Mahajan. "Market Share: Concepts, Findings and Directions for Future Research." In *Review of Marketing 1981,* edited by Ben M. Enis and Kenneth J. Roering. Chicago: American Marketing Association, 1981.

Wind, Yoram, and Vijay Mahajan. "Design Considerations in Portfolio Analysis." *Harvard Business Review* 59 (January–February 1981): 155–65.

Yavitz, Boris, and William H. Newman. *Strategy in Action: The Execution, Politics and Payoff of Business Planning.* New York: Free Press, 1982.

Yip, George S. "Gateways to Entry." *Harvard Business Review* 60 (September–October 1980): 85–92.

Index

†